BUILDING BRIDGES

BUILDING BRIDGES

The Impact of Neuropsychoanalysis on Psychoanalytic Clinical Sessions

edited by

Rosa Spagnolo

Routledge
Taylor & Francis Group

LONDON AND NEW YORK

First published 2018
by Routledge
2 Park Square, Milton Park, Abingdon, Oxon OX14 4RN

and by Routledge
711 Third Avenue, New York, NY 10017

Routledge is an imprint of the Taylor & Francis Group, an informa business

British Library Cataloguing-in-Publication Data
A catalogue record for this book is available from the British Library

Library of Congress Cataloging-in-Publication Data
A catalog record has been requested for this book

ISBN: 9781782205135 (pbk)

Typeset in Palatino
by The Studio Publishing Services Ltd
www.publishingservicesuk.co.uk
email: studio@publishingservicesuk.co.uk

CONTENTS

ABOUT THE EDITOR AND CONTRIBUTORS

The editor

Rosa Spagnolo is a child neurologist and psychiatrist, a child and adolescent psychotherapist, a psychoanalyst, Full Member of the Italian Psychoanalytical Society (SPI), and IPA Member. She is Chair of the IPA Task Force "Freud Legacy", a project to map the Freudian Heritage and register his Legacy in the UNESCO list. She works in the National Health Service on the rehabilitation of deafness, learning/speech disabilities, and developmental disorders. She is primarily an expert in the treatment of cognitive delays, autism, and child psychoses; she has been working with neuromotor and rare diseases in newborns. She is the co-founder of the Italian Psychoanalytic Dialogues. She is a passionate scholar of neuroscience. She has participated in conferences, and lectures on topics related to neuropsychiatric developmental disorder and various other psychoanalytical topics. In 2007, she published a novel, *Chantal* (Maremmi Editore, Florence), on scientific ethical issues, and has numerous professional publications to her credit.

The contributors

Tiziana Bastianini is a psychologist, psychoanalyst, training and supervising member of the Italian Psychoanalytical Society (SPI-IPA) who lives and works in Rome. She was past Scientific Secretary of SPI. Past President of the Psychoanalytic Centre of Rome (CPDR). She was Editor of the journal *Psiche*, a member of the SPI Committee on Research, and a member of the SPI Committee on Psychoanalysis and Neuroscience. She was Clinical Director of clinical services for psychotic patients in the public health service. She has directed many training projects for mental health workers and has published several papers on psychoanalytical topics.

Martin Casassus is a psychologyst graduate from Universidad Central de Chile. During the first years of his career, he worked with autistic spectrum condition (ASC), pervasive developmental disorders, and was involved in several research projects. Currently, he is a PhD student in the Division of Neuroscience and Experimental Psychology, University of Manchester, where he is working as part of the body, eye, audition, and movement (BEAM) laboratory, the time perception laboratory, and autism@manchester group. In addition, he collaborates at the Head Forward Centre. This mix of activities allows him to create bonds between the academic world and professional practice.

Francesco Castellet y Ballará is a neurologist and psychiatrist who trained in the Italian Psychoanalytical Society (SPI). He is a Full Member of the SPI/IPA. He has a great deal of experience of international organisations, having served in IPSO and the IPA as committee board member. He is also one of the organisers of several editions of Festival dei Due Mondi di Spoleto: Cinema and Psychoanalysis, Art and Psychoanalysis sections. His main areas of interest are: psychoanalysis and neuroscience, early relational trauma and adult psychopathology, pornography, and money. He is currently the psychiatric and psychoanalytic consultant at the Italian site of the European Space Agency (ESA). He is co-founder of the Italian Psychoanalytic Dialogues.

Paolo Chiari is a psychotherapist, psychoanalyst, Full Member of the Italian Psychoanalytical Society (SPI), and past Scientific Secretary of the Milan Psychoanalytic Center (CMP) "Cesare Musatti". He is the editor of several books: *Il cerchio magico* (2009), with Andreina Robutti (Milan: quaderni del CMP); *Navigando l'inconscio* (2014), with Marco Sarno (Milan: Mimesis); *La via milanese alla Psicoanalisi* (2016) (Milan: Jacabook).

Silvio Arrigo Merciai is a psychiatrist and a Member of the Italian Psychoanalytical Society (SPI/IPA). In the 1990s, he dedicated himself to studying the thought of W. R. Bion, in partnership with Parthenope Bion Talamo, the daughter of the great psychoanalyst (on this subject, they co-edited, with Franco Borgogno, two Karnac books: *Bion's Legacy to Groups* and *W. R. Bion: Between Past and Future*). The *fil rouge* in all his professional life was to keep psychoanalysis alive by— so to say—debugging it. That is why he was involved on several occasions in the analysis of the opportunities opened up by the availability of new internet tools (such as online psychotherapy). The natural alliance between neuroscience and psychoanalysis has been the main focus of his studies in the past twenty years, in co-operation with Beatrice Cannella (Merciai & Cannella, 2009).

Christian Salas is a clinical neuropsychologist and a psychoanalytic psychotherapist. He works as a lecturer and researcher at the Cognitive and Social Neuroscience Laboratory (Diego Portales University, Chile) and the Psychodynamic Psychotherapy Unit (J. H. Barak Psychiatric Institute, Chile). He is also the Director of the Diploma in Adult Neuropsychological Rehabilitation at the same university. His main interest is in understanding changes in emotion and personality after brain damage and how psychoanalytic theory and technique can be adapted to facilitate emotional adjustment. He is actively involved in the development of private and public neuropsychological rehabilitation services in Chile, in order to provide adequate short- and long-term care to individuals and families with acquired brain damage.

Mark Solms is the Director of Neuropsychology at the University of Cape Town. He is President of the South African Psychoanalytical Association and Member of the British Psychoanalytical Society and American Psychoanalytic Association. He is Research Chair of the International Psychoanalytical Association, Director of the Science Department of the American Psychoanalytic Association, and Co-Chair of the International Neuropsychoanalysis Society. He was awarded the Sigourney Prize in 2012, and Honorary Fellowship of the

American College of Psychiatrists in 2016. He has published more than 300 papers in both neuroscientific and psychoanalytic journals, and five books, including *The Brain and the Inner World* (2002), which was a bestseller translated into twelve languages. His selected writings were recently published as *The Feeling Brain* (2015). He is the editor of the forthcoming (2018) *Revised Standard Edition of the Complete Psychological Works of Sigmund Freud* (twenty-four volumes) and the *Complete Neuroscientific Works of Sigmund Freud* (four volumes).

Claudia Spadazzi, MD, is a Full Member of the Italian Psychoanalytical Society, a clinical psychologist, gynaecologist, and sexual therapist. She is a visiting Professor in Psychosomatic Gynaecology at Università Politecnica delle Marche. She has been part of the IPA Committee: IPA/IPSO, COWAP, and Public Information. She is interested in neurosciences, psychosomatics, and female psychosexuality. She is the co-founder of Italian Psychoanalytic Dialogues.

Oliver Turnbull is a neuropsychologist (and a clinical psychologist), with an interest in emotion and its many consequences for mental life. His interests include emotion-based learning, and the experience that we describe as "intuition", the role of emotion in false beliefs, especially in neurological patients, and the neuroscience of psychotherapy. He is the author of a number of scientific articles on these topics, and (together with Mark Solms) of the popular science text *The Brain and the Inner World*. For a decade, he was editor of the journal *Neuropsychoanalysis*. He is a Professor of Neuropsychology in Bangor University, where he is also Pro Vice-Chancellor (Teaching & Learning).

Maggie Zellner, PhD., LP, is the Executive Director of the Neuropsychoanalysis Foundation in New York City. She is a licensed psychoanalyst in private practice in New York City, and a member of the National Psychological Association for Psychoanalysis (NPAP). She is also a behavioural neuroscientist and received her PhD in neuropsychology at the Graduate Center of the City University of New York. She is now a member of the Adjunct Faculty at the Rockefeller University in the Laboratory of Neurobiology and Behavior, and is the editor of *Neuropsychoanalysis*. She has developed a speciality in teaching neuroscience to psychotherapists. She now takes every opportunity to link complex intrapsychic processes to underlying brain mechanisms.

Making the best of a bad job

Silvio A. Merciai

When two personalities meet, an emotional storm is created. If they make sufficient contact to be aware of each other, or even sufficient to be unaware of each other, an emotional state is produced by the conjunction of these two individuals, and the resulting disturbance is hardly likely to be regarded as necessarily an improvement on the state of affairs had they never met at all. But since they have met, and since this emotional storm has occurred, the two parties to this storm may decide to "make the best of a bad job".

Will psycho-analysts study the living mind? Or is the authority of Freud to be used as a deterrent, a barrier to studying people? The revolutionary becomes respectable – a barrier against revolution. The invasion of the animal by a germ or 'anticipation' of a means of accurate thinking, is resented by the feelings already in possession. That war has not ceased yet. (Bion, 1979, pp. 321–331)

It was towards the end of the last century, in the middle of the decade of the brain, that the long-lasting divorce between the sciences of the brain and the sciences of the mind began to fade in the light of the awesome acquisitions made possible by new neuroscientific research techniques (mainly PET and fMRI). It was at that point that some neuroscientists turned to psychoanalysis (not only to cognitive psychology), looking for a model of the mind in which their investigations could be contextualised and reframed. If some hints could be found in the works of two great neuroscientists such as Damasio (1994) and LeDoux (1996), the "official" starting date of the dialogue between neuroscience and psychoanalysis is usually fixed to 1999, with the well-known article by Kandel, "Biology and the future of psychoanalysis: a new intellectual framework for psychiatry revisited" (1999) and its unambiguous statement that: "Psychoanalysis still represents the most coherent and intellectually satisfying view of the mind" (Kandel, 1999, p. 64).

Kandel was trained at a time when psychoanalysis was dominating the American psychiatric culture, but he left psychoanalysis to devote himself to the study of what has been, since then, called the "biology of the mind": thanks to his knowledge in both fields, he indicated a number of areas where neuroscience and psychoanalysis could and should co-operate, called for a convergence of neuroscience, cognitive psychology, and psychoanalysis, and urged the psychoanalytic institutions to a decisive turning-point towards a science-based, verifiable, and multi-disciplinary development, and a consequent deep revision of the methods and models of the training of new analysts. Apart from some voices, authoritative but isolated, such as those of Kernberg and Fonagy, psychoanalytic institutions' reply remained for a long time relatively uninterested or intolerant. And such remains, in my opinion, after many years, even today, as demonstrated by the recent issue of the Italian psychoanalytical journal, *Psicoterapia e Scienze Umane*, in which the editor, Paolo Migone (2016), hosts the results of research on "What remains of psychoanalysis", carried out by interviewing several authors belonging to the Italian and international psychoanalytic world with a twelve-item questionnaire in which one of the questions actually focused on the relationship between neuroscience and psychoanalysis (How do you assess the recent developments in neuroscience and neurobiology compared to psychoanalysis?). The responses (but not all respondents chose to grapple with this question) were sometimes clearly negative, such as, for example,

> I look at the developments in neuroscience and neurobiology as among the most fascinating journeys that the human mind can do, and [like] astrophysics they have nothing to do with psychoanalysis. (Antonino Ferro, in Migone, 2016, p. 446)

Some neuroscientific discoveries and theories are very interesting, but, up to now, psychoanalytic practice found no use of them. It is as if a biologist expert in batrachology wished to apply quantum mechanics to his field! It could be correct in theory, but in practice it would be a nonsense. Very often, the invocation, by some analysts, of neuroscientific terms or concepts is a ploy to appear up-to-date, "modern", but often no convincing relationship can be found between clinical practice and neuroscientific findings. I find it more interesting that renowned neuroscientists, such as Edelmann, Kandel, and Rizzolatti, value the Freudian model. Psychoanalysis can give to neurobiology more than it does the opposite. (Sergio Benvenuto, in Migone, 2016, pp. 375–376)

Other answers to the previously mentioned questionnaire seem to show more interest, but with many caveats, such as those of Ammanniti, Bollas, Scarfone, Fonagy, Target, Eagle, Lingiardi, and Lichtenberg, among others; only few responses show a direct appreciation of the dialogue, such as those of Bohleber, Roussillon, Bucci, and Ferruta. No responses directly imply that psychoanalysis should refine its theory thanks to co-operation with the neurosciences: quite the opposite of what is stated by some neuroscientists following in the footsteps of Kandel, chiefly among them Damasio (2012), who has written:

Similarity of goals aside, psychoanalysis and neuroscience are distinct fields of inquiry. The techniques used by psychoanalysis to investigate the human mind and its sub agencies are materially different and more circumscribed than the large range of techniques available to neuroscience. One might add that such a difference is entirely to be expected. After all, neuroscience deals with every aspect of the structure and animation of all nervous systems, human and not, while psychoanalysis concentrates on one process and product of the human brain. The scopes of the two fields are clearly not comparable, but that is not a hurdle. On the contrary, it is apparent that the diverse armamentarium of neuroscience can be brought to bear on the specific problems of human mind processing that psychoanalysis has been approaching, and will likely explore further in the future. There is a natural alliance here and it is already at work. (pp. 591–592)

An analogous positive appreciation—not surprisingly—has been taken by some scholars working in the field of neuroscience, but also having training in psychoanalysis (two Italian names stand out,

Alberini and Mancia). The psychoanalytic mainstream is still delaying developing models, or theories, showing the results of a real and fruitful dialogue between the neurosciences and psychoanalysis (the work of Schore and Fonagy and those who were inspired by their proposals are, perhaps, currently the more brilliant exceptions). The task proposed by Kandel—to abandon metapsychology and, in a sense, to rewrite a psychoanalytic theory based on the biology of the mind—is maybe proving to be a kind of mission impossible for the current generation of psychoanalysts.

The neuro-psychoanalytic movement, founded and championed with great determination by Solms (actually another scholar trained both in neurosciences and psychoanalysis), has been, and still is, the most comprehensive and systematic attempt to establish and nurture the dialogue between the two disciplines bound together by the hyphen "-" (which was later dropped):

> It seems entirely appropriate to reconsider whether we might now attempt to map the neurological basis of what we have learnt in psychoanalysis about the structure and functions of the mind, using neuroscientific methods available to us today. Freud, in our opinion, would have considered this a welcome and wholly legitimate development of the work that he pioneered. . . . The interface between psychoanalysis and neuroscience is a rather dialectical one. As analysts, we may learn something new about the brain that seems relevant to psychoanalysis. We may think about it, keep it at the back of our minds, entertain the possibility, but above all we test it psychoanalytically as well as investigate its clinical usefulness. (Solms & Turnbull, 2016, pp. 17–26)

My purpose in this brief foreword cannot be to explore the richness of the contributions made over the years by Solms (see, at least, Solms, 2015) and his followers, or to try to draw any inferences about the influence it has exerted on the psychoanalytic culture. Actually, the movement went through complicated stages in its evolution: the progressive centrality given to the theories developed by Panksepp has, for some time, ended up overshadowing the contributions of other scholars, weakening the many voices' dialogue feature that characterised the onset of the movement. The journal *Neuropsychoanalysis* has had delays and blockages in the continuity of its publication and has struggled to retain its readers and authors. At the beginning, in particular, the almost exclusive reference to Freudian doctrine attracted justifiable criticism, in accordance with the words of Michels (2010), for example, Neuropsychoanalysis was a discipline more orientated towards showing that many of the theories of Freud were correct (as argued in a well-known paper by Solms (2004), translated into several languages) than to forming a bridge to contemporary psychoanalysis. But, thanks to the hard work done by Zellner while leading the International Neuropsychoanalysis Society and the intellectual vitality of the various conferences annually held, the neuropsychoanalytic culture has gradually grown up and broadened its horizons (opening, for example, to the discoveries of Gallese and Damasio) and it is today the natural ground on which to cultivate hope for the dialogue between neuroscience and psychoanalysis and the achievement of consilience, as Kandel (2011) suggested:

> My overriding concern is to try to bridge the gap between biology and psychoanalysis. Biologists of the brain are interested in understanding how the mind works, and it's difficult for them to do that unless they have a nuanced understanding of mental processes. I think we've got to get to a phase in which we … focus in on a few paradigmatic questions, in which the first one is, "Does it work?" Can we localize different mental functions in the different regions of the brain? And then we need to follow the changes that occur with different psychotherapeutic experiences. And from that as a base we can really develop a new synthesis, much as Freud tried to do in 1895 with the Project for a Scientific Psychology, but at a completely new level, a synthesis between biology and psychoanalytic treatment. . . . I think [the dream of consilience] is wonderful. I think that's what's necessary. It's a dream, but that's what we live for. (pp. 159–165)

You end up, almost always, when writing about the dialogue between psychoanalysis and neuroscience and trying to strike a balance about the possible fruitfulness of it, with quoting a widely known study by Pulver (2003), who, chronicling his experience as a psychoanalyst, distinguished the astonishing relevance of neuroscience to psychoanalytic theory from the equally astonishing irrelevance of neuroscience to psychoanalytic technique. Actually, it no longer looks sustainable to ignore the rich contributions that the neurosciences—though still only at the foot of the mountain, according to a neat analogy of Kandel's—have made to the understanding of the mental mechanisms that govern our feelings and emotions, our continuous decision-making processes, the architecture of our motivations, the genesis and management of all relationships and socialisation processes, the very foundations on which thrives our ethical world, our illusion of free will, and especially, to the great satisfaction of the psychoanalytic world, the absolute primacy of unconscious mechanisms in our mental life.[1] That is why the reference to Pulver's paper is generally meant to assert that neuroscience could even turn out to be useful for the elaboration of psychoanalytic theory (actually stuff for academic scholars), but it certainly would be an unnecessary burden for the culture of the psychoanalyst who works with real patients in his consulting room. Most of the authors believe that the neurosciences cannot inspire us in the conduct of a clinical case in a psychoanalytical (or a psychoanalytically orientated) setting.

I disagree openly from this position (Merciai & Cannella, 2009), while recognising that a long way still has to be travelled by psychoanalysis in order to fully realise the usefulness of that dialogue. On closer inspection, I also feel that the idea that something useful for our theory could be irrelevant to our technique is epistemologically untenable, as if theory and technique were completely unrelated to one another, but psychoanalysis is, so to say, a peculiar world if (limiting myself to one authoritative example) even such a representative author as Sandler, former president of the IPA, could argue some years ago (Sandler, 1983) that the official theory and the technical features that every psychoanalyst implements, in the privacy of his consulting room, are not closely congruent.

That is why I follow with keen interest the authors that offer clinical examples and try to build theories for the technique that can disprove the negativistic tradition that goes back to Pulver.

I conclude by briefly mentioning three examples.

1. The masterly paper by Yovell and colleagues (2015), in which they discuss a case in the context of the controversy "the case against neuropsychoanalysis", begun, in 2007, by Blass and Carmeli who, in further papers, have argued that the interest in neuroscience is not only irrelevant, but also harmful for psychoanalysis.

2. The statements by Alberini (2015) on the usability of the new acquisitions in the field of memory reconsolidation:

I believe that knowing the temporal dynamics and mechanisms underlying memory retrieval, stabilization, destabilization, processing, and updating with new associations will significantly aid in designing more precise and individuated treatments in psychoanalytic settings. For example, this knowledge can help determine when to intervene, what type of information should be used, and what modalities are most effective. (p. 318)

3.   The wise remarks by Ponsi (2016) about the opportunity to 'keep the brain in mind'

Rather than individual acquisitions, therefore, at this stage, I would give importance to that sort of internal state of mind at work reorganisation that I have summarised in the expression "keeping the brain in mind". There is an important point I want to stress in this respect. In order to make possible a fruitful interaction with the neurobiological data in the mind of the analyst, it is necessary to get rid of the psychogenic perspective, or at least loosen ties with psychodynamic explanations. . . . Psychoanalysis must be very cautious in advancing aetiological hypotheses and in explaining why a disorder, or a mental dysfunctional organisation, takes place, and must devote itself to its specific task, which is to understand from within the processes by which we organise the states of mental suffering (. . . the how rather than the why) and to develop a narrative as much as possible consistent with the neurobiological correlates of psychopathology and the mental state conditions of which it has clinical experience. (translated by the Editor for this edition)

This volume represents a significant step forward in this direction, because it directly addresses the issue of the clinical relevance of the neurosciences to psychoanalysis by comparing the theoretical writings of some very influential representatives of the neuropsychoanalytic world with some psychoanalytic vignettes that are discussed with the aim to show the fruitfulness of the dialogue between neuroscience and psychoanalysis. Our readers will evaluate whether this goal has been achieved.

Note

1.   Unlocking and exploring the topic of the unconscious mind is currently the main area of shared interest between psychoanalysis and

neuroscience, as shown, for example, by the publication of the book *The Unconscious* (Leuzinger-Bohleber, Arnold, & Solms, Eds., 2016) and by the three conferences "Unlocking the Unconscious: Exploring the Undiscovered Self" hosted by the Nour Foundation (www.nour foundation.com/unlocking-the-unconscious.html).

References

Alberini, C. M. (2015). Commentary on touch. *Journal of American Psychoanalytic Association, 63*(2): 316–330.

Bion, W. R. (1979). Making the best of a bad job. In: F. Bion (Ed.), *Clinical Seminars and Other Works* (pp. 321–331). London: Karnac, 1994.

Blass, R. B., & Carmeli, Z. (2007). The case against neuropsychoanalysis: on fallacies underlying psychoanalysis' latest scientific trend and its negative impact on psychoanalytic discourse. *International Journal of Psychoanalysis, 88:* 19–40.

Blass, R. B., & Carmeli, Z. (2015). Further evidence for the case against neuropsychoanalysis: how Yovell, Solms, and Fotopoulou's response to our critique confirms the irrelevance and harmfulness to psychoanalysis of the contemporary neuroscientific trend. *International Journal of Psychoanalysis, 96:* 1555–1573.

Damasio, A. (1994). *Descartes' Error: Emotion, Reason and the Human Brain.* New York: Avon Books.

Damasio, A. (2012). Neuroscience and psychoanalysis: a natural alliance. *Psychoanalytic Review, 99*(4): 591–592.

Kandel, E. R. (1999). Biology and the future of psychoanalysis: a new intellectual framework for psychiatry revisited. *American Journal of Psychiatry, 156:* 505–524.

Kandel, E. R. (2011). "Nitty-gritty issues": an interview with Eric R. Kandel. In: P. L. Rudnytsky (Ed.), *Rescuing Psychoanalysis from Freud and Other Essays in Re-vision* (pp. 159–165). London: Karnac.

LeDoux, J. (1996). *The Emotional Brain.* New York: Simon and Schuster.

Leuzinger-Bohleber, M., Arnold, S., & Solms, M. (Eds.) (2016). *The Unconscious: A Bridge Between Psychoanalysis and Cognitive Neuroscience.* Abingdon: Routledge.

Merciai, S. A., & Cannella, B. (2009). *La Psicoanalisi nelle Terre di Confine.* Milan: Cortina.

Michels, R. (2010). Ten years later, the Philoctetes Center for the multidisciplinary study of the imagination. *Psychoanalysis and Neuroscience,* https://youtube/zlkliGaIBQI.

Migone, P. (2016). *Psicoterapia e Scienze Umane, Numero speciale del cinquantesimo anno*. Milan: FrancoAngeli.

Ponsi, M. (2016). Trasformazioni psichiche, plasticità neurobiologica. Se l'analista ha in mente il cervello. www.spiweb.it/neuroscienze-autori/7638-ponsi-m-2016-trasformazioni-psichiche-plasticita-neuro biologica-se-l-analista-ha-in-mente-il-cervello (last entry 30 May 2017).

Pulver, S. E. (2003). On the astonishing clinical irrelevance of neuroscience. *Journal of the American Psychoanalytic Association, 51*(3): 755–772.

Sandler, J. (1983). Reflections on some relations between psychoanalytic concepts and psychoanalytic practice. *International Journal of Psychoanalysis, 64*: 35–45.

Solms, M. (2004). Freud returns. *Scientific American, 290*: 82–88.

Solms, M. (2015). *The Feeling Brain: Selected Papers on Neuropsychoanalysis*. London: Karnac.

Solms, M., & Turnbull, O. H. (2016). What is neuropsychoanalysis? In: S. Weigel & G. Scharbert (Eds), *A Neuro-Psychoanalytical Dialogue for Bridging Freud and the Neurosciences* (pp. 17–26). Switzerland: Springer.

Yovell, Y., Solms, M., & Fotopoulou, A. (2015). The case for neuropsychoanalysis: why a dialogue with neuroscience is necessary but not sufficient for psychoanalysis. *International Journal of Psychoanalysis, 96*: 1515–1553.

PART I

NEUROPSYCHOANALYSIS FROM DREAM TO CASE STUDIES

CHAPTER ONE

Gateways into the dream

Rosa Spagnolo

The past century, which was marked by *The Interpretation of Dreams* (Freud, 1900a), and this one have witnessed an impressive production of psychoanalytic work centred upon dreams and dreaming. Eminent representatives from the psychoanalytic world have produced relevant essays upon this topic, enlarging, and sometimes radically transforming, the original Freudian theory. In parallel to this psychoanalytic corpus, there has been a gradual and increasing emergence of other studies related to the mechanism involved in the production of dreams and to the area of cognition present in it. The discovery of REM/non-REM sleep in the 1950s has boosted both neurophysiological research and the study of the anatomic correlation of sleep–dream; also, it has definitely strengthened the neuropsychological research that looks into the mechanisms and processes of the brain/mental activity made evident by the dream. Therefore, we can say that the current interweaving of these three disciplines—psychoanalysis, neuroanatomy/physiology, and neuropsychology—does describe the dream in the three dimensions that contribute to its production; in other words, the subjective dimension, the process, and the scaffolding that holds it. Each aspect—subjective, procedural, and neurological dimension—produces just a partial vision which would never sufficiently account for the mythical (Cassirer, 1959) and religious (Mancia, 1988)[1] dimension of dream that, according to psychoanalysis, "testifies to the patient's history, reveals the geography of the unconscious and gives meaning to experience" (Civitarese, 2013, p. 10). At present, different works related to the above-mentioned disciplines give the dream a central role in a number of processes whose internal mechanisms take place far beyond the subject's awareness, such as in affect regulation, information processing, adaptation to stress, problem solving, and in the consolidation and reconsolidation of memory. We could say that the dream is the hinge between the conscious and the unconscious, between biological and mental processes, at which it is possible to look from different angles.

> And what do we dream about? We dream about our most immediate concerns: our dreams include attempts to resolve conflict, to self-regulate, to regulate affect, to envision and move developmentally, to fortress threatened patterns of organization, to consolidate new experience, and to integrate and enhance new learning. (Fosshage, 2013, p. 253)

Freud (1900a) defines the issues that are important enough to enter our dreams like this: "We only bother to dream of things which have given us cause for reflection in the daytime" (p. 174). On this basis, I propose some reflections upon what is incorporated into the dream, what we find apart from this input, and, in parallel to this, where this input leads us.

"Father, don't you see I'm burning?"

The preliminaries to this model dream were as follows. A father had been watching beside his child's sickbed for days and nights on end. After the child had died, he went into the next room to lie down, but left the door open so that he could see from his bedroom into the room in which his child's body was laid out, with tall candles standing round it. An old man had been engaged to keep watch over it, and sat beside the body murmuring prayers. After a few hours' sleep, the father had a dream that his child was standing beside his bed, caught him by the arm and whispered to him reproachfully, "Father, don't you see I'm burning?" He woke up, noticed a bright glare of light from the next room, hurried into it, and found that the old watchman had dropped off to sleep and that the wrappings and one of the arms of his beloved child's dead body had been burned by a lighted candle that had fallen on them. (Freud, 1900a, p. 509)

Through this dream, placed at the beginning of Chapter VII of *The Interpretation of Dreams*, (1900a), Freud seems to hide some sort of isomorphism between the thoughts during the waking and the content of the dream. It is the awakening that confirms it; some part of what he was dreaming is really taking place. This is the explanation that Freud gives (in the first part of Chapter VII):

The glare of light shone through the open door into the sleeping man's eyes and led him to the conclusion which he would have arrived at if he had been awake, namely that a candle had fallen over and set something alight in the neighborhood of the body. It is even possible that he had felt some concern when he went to sleep as to whether the old man might not be incompetent to carry out his task. (Freud, 1900a, p. 509)

Therefore, some of the father's thoughts regarding the watching over of the deceased son had entered the dream and, through sensory excitation of the retina, had provoked the awakening. Freud concludes:

Here we are facing a dream which does not pose any problem of interpretation, one whose meaning is openly given from the start, and we can see it still keeps the essential characteristics through which the dream remarkably differs from our waking life thoughts and arouses our need for an explanation. (Freud, 1900a, p. 510)

The main characteristics of the dream are analysed over the chapter through the elements that have contributed to its production, that is to say, verbal remnants from a past or present speech, whose very words constitute the dream script, the desire to see his son alive once again, unwanted representations that ask for figurability, the continuity of waking life thoughts during the dream, a recent impression that is connected to a number of preceding ones, and, finally, after having looked into the four sources of desire, he introduces the importance of the waking life remnants:

I shall follow the same line of thought in now turning to consider those psychical instigations to dreaming, left over from waking life, which are other than wishes ... If we wish to classify the thought-impulses which persist in sleep, we may divide them into the following groups: (1) what has not been carried to a conclusion during the day owing to some chance hindrance; (2) what has not been dealt with owing to the insufficiency of our intellectual power – what is unsolved; (3) what has been rejected and suppressed during the daytime. To these we must add (4) a powerful group consisting of what has been set in action in our Ucs. by the activity of the preconscious in the course of the day; and finally (5) the group of daytime impressions which are indifferent and have for that reason not been dealt with. (Freud, 1900a, p. 554)

We shall now see the way these physical instigations to dreaming have been investigated by empirical research, both psychoanalytical and not; in particular, we are going to take into consideration some research related to depression, addiction, and trauma. It must be remembered that the methods applied to analyse the incorporation of daytime residue into dreams differ, depending on the kind of research that is carried out. Those generally used are pre-sleep simulation (through images and film settings), sensory stimulation (the production of environmental sounds and smells directly during the dream), and subjective identification *post hoc*, before oneiric memory.

First, I shall point out Nielsen and colleagues' research on the timing of this input (daytime residues in the dream) as a generic premise on dreams rather than the single topics.

By analysing 470 students' dreams, Nielsen and colleagues (2004) described the double-time process by which daytime residue is incorporated into dreams. There is a first time, called day-residue effect, in which the main characteristics of a daily event pass directly into the dream, and the dream-lag effect, in which the specific event comes into the dream later, after about a week. Moreover, in the aftermath of this work, Nielsen and Stenstrom (2005) conducted a review of similar studies, pointing out that dreams do not portray the entire sequence of episodic memories, their fragmentation being much more common instead. So, these authors suggest that the dream should propose a sort of subjective "here and now" which produces a coherent and continuing narrative, due to the autonoetic awareness[2] of the dream:

Episodic fragments (characters, settings, objects) and patterns (for example, emotion sequences), as well as semantic information, undergo binding over time such that illusions of a first-person perspective and a sense of the continuous present are maintained. (Nielsen & Stenstrom, 2015, p. 1287)

The dream, then, seems to talk to us in the present time and: "present tense is the one in which the desire is represented as fulfilled" (Freud, 1900a, p. 535). The present is the time of the dream that unfolds through the incorporation of the day residues.

What gets into the dream, and what we are able to find beyond this input

Domhoff applies his hypothesis of embodied simulation (Domhoff, 2011) to studying a widower's dreams of his deceased wife; 143 dreams which were written down over twenty-two years of his widowerhood.[3] Domhoff reaches the conclusion that the principal themes of his dreams—his wife's health condition and his relationship with her while she was still alive—are consistent with the concerns about life and marriage present in the reflection notes written by the same widower during waking life. These themes happen to be enacted, dramatised in the form of figurative embodiments related to his thoughts of seeing her alive, of being reassured and comforted by her presence, of going back to the past time lived together. Alongside this embodied simulation of the dream, Domhoff finds other images he defines as unrealistic, which require further studies in order to be better differentiated from the proper figurative embodiments, because the so-called unrealistic embodiments might be the result of some deficit or cognitive malfunctioning during the dream.

The "unrealistic" elements (which seem to be consistent with those defined by Blechner, 2013, as bizarre or irrational)[4] are 104 out of a total of 143 dreams, a significant majority which should be considered within the mechanism of representation and, therefore, of the transformation that the daytime residue is due to face (concerns and conceptions for the author). Even more than the reading of the 143 dreams, it draws our attention the fact that the bizarre figures (unrealistic elements) are almost always related to the disease that led to the loss of his wife. In other words, these bizarre elements are those directly related to the difficulty of mourning, which, through the paradox of these bizarre figures, combines the present time (the desire to see her alive right now) with the past time (the autonoetic awareness of her death).

Let us go back to the daytime residues and their embodiment in dreams through events which imply a high traumatic impact, such as the attack to the Twin Towers, or the war in the Balkans.

Hartmann and Brezler (2008) collected 880 dreams of forty-four people,[5] each of them providing a total of twenty dreams in the following way, ten dreams prior to the traumatic event and ten following it. The aim of the experiment was to assess if the traumatic event might provoke any changes in the "Central Dream Imagery": "A contextualizing image or central image is a striking, arresting, or compelling image—not simply a story—but an image that stands out by virtue of being especially powerful, vivid, bizarre, or detailed" (Hartmann & Brezler, 2008, p. 214).

A central image is clear to distinguish by the fact of being particularly powerful due to its tie with the emotional system. The results were expected to show an increase of intensity of the central dream imagery, and they were confirmed as such. What is more, it was discovered that in the dreams there were neither images of what had been directly seen, nor explicit images of high buildings, aeroplanes, towers, etc. Notably, those images reflecting the idea of being attacked had increased in number. That means that the dreams were recording the emotional state of being afraid of being attacked, of being a potential victim of violence, and this was portrayed in images of various kind.

According to the authors' analysis, we can say that the images present in the dreams were by no means a reflection of what had been previously seen, but had been created from scratch, responding to a daytime emotional request. Thus, here again, this study reintroduces what has already been stated many times by many authors, that there exists a strong continuity between the concerns (emotions) from waking life and what comes up during a dream, going through the stages of mind wandering and day-dreaming (widely reviewed in Domhoff & Fox, 2015). The real news, for some of us, is that these emotionally charged waking thoughts are not portrayed, and embodied in the dream following the linear laws of a figurative copy of reality that reflects the original.

One way to investigate even further the entering of daily experiences into the world of dreams is the one carried out by the research group of Belgrade, 2004–2005, about the post-trauma dreams of subjects who had been recruited right after the Balkans War. This is a widely discussed study that has been presented on several occasions (e.g., Hau et al., 2013; Varvin et al., 2012).

There were fifty subjects selected who reported different "war related stress factors".[6] Out of these, twenty-five had developed the pre-eminent symptoms of PTSD (experimental group) and twenty-five subjects did not show symptoms of PTSD (reference group).

Sixty dream reports (thirty from each group) were collected in the dream laboratory and analysed with the Moser method and the Psychoanalytic Enunciation Analysis (PEA).[7]

Both methods allowed a detailed analysis of the many elements present in the dreams, giving great importance to the interruption of sleep. Notably, the collection and writing of the dream reports generated anxiety and even nightmares in many of the operators assigned to this task because the contents were closely linked to situations of torture, murder, dismemberment, and violent decisions to be taken in conditions of appalling outrage which were present in both the figurative dream and the real, true accounts reported during the interviews.

In short, the analysis carried out showed that the group with PTSD had a greater frequency of dream interruption, a lowering of their capacity to create correlates among affections, and a lack of involvement, either reciprocal or interactive. A sense of destruction and deterioration was frequently present, together with a strong desire for annihilation, accompanied by difficult feelings of helplessness. In the control group, however, the principle of a greater involvement and the ability to find a solution to the conflict was prevalent.

Hau and colleagues (2013) presented the analysis of subject 230. He is a Serb who had been captured and tortured in Croatia. On being interviewed, he says he has the recurrent image of a man who is a prisoner and is threatened to be slaughtered while he is watching the scene. The next night, in the two dreams collected in the laboratory (during two enforced REM awakenings) he talks about "the slaughtering of lambs" and about him while "picking mushrooms". These two dreams reports were not chosen by the authors to be analysed, as they were looking for other kinds of dreams (replica dreams). These dreams usually keep a narrative structure far richer in themes closely related to traumatic war experiences, which might enable the authors to question, and eventually find out, whether there is a real difference between the fact of re-experiencing the trauma and dreaming about it.

Replica dreams are indicators with a very limited possibility to transform the dream, being a quantum of emotion and affect that exceeds this capacity; whereas dreams like the one about the slaughtering of lambs might represent, within the subject's economy, both dreaming and re-experiencing the trauma in a more accessible mode; a clear advantage for the dreamer and the analyst! On the other hand, through this single image, which is neither a compliant copy nor a bizarre one, the emotion–affects related to the horror of the trauma appear into the dreams transformed by oneiric figuration.

What Hartmann and Brezler argue (2008), about the power of a central image charged with affects related to the emotional intensity of the first experienced emotion, can clearly be seen in all its iconic explanatory power through the image of "the slaughtered lambs". It is possible to say that: *strongly invested experiences can be incorporated into the dream through either a compliant copy (replica dream) or through a non-compliant copy of the original, but still keeping the same emotional intensity of the original.* Compliant copy dreams can be found in highly traumatic situations (and, thus, charged with negative emotions) as well as in those situations affected with positive emotions, such as desire (no one has ever investigated the dreams of lovers, but we do have several dream reports regarding the desires of addicts).

Dreams that are isomorphic to the reality of a specific desire for drugs are called "drug dreams" (Colace, 2014). Their common characteristic is the direct figuration of the desired event: drug craving (Colace, 2010). Such dreams have a very simple content that usually refers to what is lived during waking life, that is, buying, manipulating, seeking, or taking drugs. Just like children's dreams, these are very simple, concise and brief, they lack bizarre elements or any covering up of the satisfaction of desire and the subject has an active role in its search (Colace, 2014).

The emotions attached to these dreams are generally those of pleasure and relief due to the use of the substance. Dream reports about drug refusal are included in the psychoanalytical literature, but are less frequent than those in which the drug is being searched for or used (Colace, 2014). Therefore, the desire and its fulfilment seem to directly permeate the manifest content of these dreams:

> The most striking psychological characteristic of the process of dreaming: a thought, and as a rule a thought of something that is wished, is objectified in the dream, is represented as a scene, or as it seems to us, is experienced. (Freud, 1900a, p. 534)

Thanks to the development of oneiric figuration, in these cases of direct movement of the waking thought into dream, it is possible to access useful information about any changes taking place in the course of psychotherapy. Most researchers who deal with addiction are already looking into these matters in order to better apply what they can learn from them (Colace, 2014).

Similar purpose has inspired research into therapeutic changes in depression (Fischmann et al., 2013) that can be followed up through the dream analysis of a patient undergoing psychoanalytical treatment. This research, which compares the dream reports from the beginning of the treatment to those at the beginning of the third year of analysis, provides significant evidence of the changes in the relational models (self–object), of an increase in the range of action of the dream-subject, as well as of an increase in the emotional spectrum (Fischmann et al., 2012).[8]

The possibility of following up these kinds of changes in the treatment of depression, in the same therapeutic clinic, through oneiric expression, had already been tried and verified by Cartwright et al. (1984). The result of her work (the twenty cases analysed reported depression of the spouse following divorce) shows that daily emotional concerns are represented in dreams in a different way when the patient's depression is in remission, compared to those patients still experiencing the symptoms. The patients who were not in remission showed a lower capacity to link affects to memory and to experience emotions in their dreaming. That is to say, their dreams did not present the incorporation of their ex-spouse into a memory web associated to it and, in waking life, they continued to show the same emotional difficulties connected to the divorce. Cartwright's conclusion comes really close to Bion's idea about the transformation of affects by dreams, with a relapse in waking life. Cartwright argues that the dream content is linked to the dreamer's continuous emotional concerns and contributes to regulating mood excitation when the affects are kept within a specific quantum. If the affect to be regulated is too high or too low for it to be linked to the relative memory, this dream function will fail to operate. This failure blocks the transforming process of the emotions during dreaming and, consequently, during waking life. In other words, the patients who were not in remission were not able to use dream to regulate (digest and transform, for Bion) affects which remained in mood excitation.

The concept of daytime residue that is incorporated into dreams is very wide. Certainly, our own emotional and affective world is directly incorporated into dreams, but not always through images that are isomorphic to reality (compliant copy of episodic memory). Examples of unrealistic images are part of our patients' oneiric baggage, and also our own. It is these unrealistic images that excite our interest, since they exceed the common sense of iconic representation and stray into the representation of affects.

What do we find in the dream?

A is a little girl about nine years old. It is two years since she started psychoanalytic psychotherapy, attending sessions twice a week, as she presents sudden and frequent faints due to a heart rhythm block, and that is why she has had an on demand pacemaker implanted. She is calm and quiet, showing no signs of apprehension about her symptom. The pacemaker battery is regularly checked as it comes into use quite frequently. In the session prior to an appointment to have the battery and the generator replaced, she talks about a dream:

> I was here with you. We were not drawing with the usual black pencils, instead we had so many colourful pencils at hand and we were having a great time drawing. At the end of the session I put everything away in its place. Every pencil found its place back in the box and everything was in order again. I went away happily because I had been able to leave everything in order for the first time.

The following day, during her appointment to have her pacemaker checked, she is sent back home without having her battery and generator replaced, as had been expected. Her mother calls to tell me that everything is all right; apparently, everything is back to normal now, the pacemaker has never been turned on and so the battery is not used up and it seems that everything is in order.

I have wondered what kind of knowledge might convey that dream: maybe a body knowledge non-accessible to the waking consciousness. Therefore, an unconscious knowledge, one linked to unconscious transformations (also therapeutic) we ignored, but which the patient had recorded from somewhere and the dream proposed. What did it propose? A little box of colourful pencils put back into order. This is the dream's banal manifest content, but was that all? From a formal point of view (the scenario representation, the articulation of image and figurative narrative), A's dream (pencils in order), as well as that one of patient 230 (slaughtered lambs), or the many dreams of "Ed", are all perfectly coherent with the construction of the oneiric scene. If they were to be examined without any reference to the dreamer's account, the context in which they were developed, the time when they were produced, that is, if they were separated from the subject, they would be banal. What makes them less banal?

Once the daytime residue (emotions, thoughts, and concerns we are not always aware of) have been incorporated into the dream, they start to dance from one cerebral area (Zellner, 2013) to the other, getting rid of some elements (sensory de-afferentation and inhibition of the executive functions),[9] being enriched by others, creating new links from memory fragments (Payne & Nadel, 2004; Schredl, 2010), speaking in the present while recruiting old memories and, in the end, they turn up transformed and impossible to recognise when remembering the dream.

The dream embodies all these interactive processes among cerebral structures that exchange signals (bits of information) throughout sleep. The dream process fragments, disjoints, repairs, and generates new scenarios. We are not to know any of this except through some remaining fragments of memory in awakening, or in some dramatic way when the machine gets partially stuck, creating the same images recurrently or causing the awakening. Those few memories we manage to have, no matter how banal they might look, are a precious gift. Not only do they indicate the unconscious way followed by the daytime residues in the creation of new scenes, but they also allow us to become aware of the emotional and affective values that dominate our inner world that would otherwise remain buried in this endless hard night work we know nothing about. If the rule is to forget the dream, next to the question "Why do we dream?" we should add a further question, "Why do we remember dreams?"

In 1951, Fromm talked about dream images as if they were a language in which we can express inner experience, as if they were sensory experiences, data which have been widely confirmed by neuroscience, and to this Fosshage, 1997, adds:

Images do not get transformed or disguised one into another on the way between the manifest content and the latent one, otherwise they are chosen for their evocative power in the same way we choose the words with which we prepare a speech. (p. 443)

Images are not to be translated, primary process towards secondary process; they must keep the metaphor open even when the dream account does not sound logical or coherent. Every bizarre and irrational element (Blechner, 2013) of the dream exactly characterises and differentiates it from day-dreaming and mind wandering (Fox et al., 2013). Although the first and the latter share the same type of cognition (Domhoff & Fox, 2015), in my opinion, they are not assimilable. Blechner, for this reason, talks about either the grammar of irrationality (Blechner, 2005), which characterises the cognition of the dream with respect to the awakening, or about the disjunctive cognition (Blechner, 2005, 2013).[10]

What appears in waking consciousness presents itself as a synthesis (different cerebral systems function during waking life, operating a continuous synthesis of the perceptual data in order to focus our attention only upon some data, leaving out the greatest part of the sensorial input to be able to respond just to some of them), but, in dreaming, where there is no need for an executive output, everything can coexist and be simultaneously figurative. Bizarre elements, hypersensory deployments, together with intense emotional reactions, are allowed into the dreaming consciousness owing to the loosened tie with acute prefrontal instances. In this way, the dreams can create in each of us every night what artists are able to do in daytime.

Hobson (2013) calls these dream formations "incomplete cognitions"; Freud (1900) calls them "intermediate and composite structures." I call these dream formations "interobjects" (Blechner, 2001). Rather than focus on what they are not (not complete condensations), I would prefer to focus on what they are (new creations derived from blends of other objects). (Blechner, 2013, p. 172)

How can these new objects come to life? Needless to say, the research on memory and dreaming becomes of great value in order to continue with the reflection of what we can find in the dream that remains from those waking thought impulses that originally enhanced it.

With regard to memory consolidation and reconsolidation, and particularly with reference to the feebleness of memory at the moment of being recalled, Alberini (2011, 2014) writes:

> At least two, non-mutually exclusive hypotheses have been proposed to explain the function of reconsolidation. According to one, memory becomes labile because through reconsolidation new information is integrated into the background of the past, thus allowing the memory to be updated (Lewis, 1979; Sara, 2000a; Dudai, 2004) (Sara, 2006). The other proposes that memory reconsolidates in order to become stronger and longer lasting. (Alberini, 2011, p. 2)

Admittedly, studies about memory consolidation/reconsolidation are full of doubts and hypotheses for the time being (review in Balderas et al., 2015; Ecker, 2015). This fact regards not only the destination of memory in the dream-sleep (Paller & Voss, 2004) but, in a wider approach, also the making of memory (Kandell, Edelman, and Damasio have dealt with these topics) and its storage and conservation over time.

If, as has been asserted in the past by Winson (1985), the dream allows memory reorganisation with the different contributions of non-REM and REM sleep, dream should show us something about this organisation that involves the present and also the past. What is more, the dream could be the only way to access the "implicit memory in its double procedural and emotional–affective dimension referred to the primary mother–child relationship experience" (Mancia, 2006, p. 630).

Conclusion

"Dreams are never occupied with minor details" (Freud, 1900a, p. 586).

The challenges to face in order to grasp its whole comprehension are still numerous and many hypotheses still have to be tested, confirmed, and consolidated in the psychoanalytical world as well as in the neuroscientific world.

Here are some examples.

It would be really useful for the treatment of pathologies where dissociation (Bromberg, 2011) and lack of memory registration (Yovell, 2014) are prevalent to be able to "read" in the sleep production the double contribution coming from the two hemispheres that take part simultaneously in the making of dreams so as to find what, in waking life, is not accessible because it is dominated by the reductive synthesis operated by the conscious mind (thought as the immediate product of defence).

Consolidation and reconsolidation of memory: the dream (or, better said, the oneiric REM and non-REM sleep product) performs this continuous retranscription of memory; the dream recall would have an added value of the memory track vitalisation (i.e., of momentary memory restart), which would open up a way for its transformation. Besides, it would communicate to the dreamer what would otherwise remain unconscious, that is to say impossible to access from consciousness (we know about the unconscious through its derivatives—dream, symptoms, and lapses).

I shall not talk about the link between the unconscious and the dream, that is, about the very place where dream has its origin. The dream is unconscious and carries the signs of the work of the unconscious. The day residue acts as a hinge between the waking consciousness and the dream consciousness: functioning just like a zip, it holds the two strings that, wedging into each other, manage to close some scenarios (access to reality) and to open further new ones (access to the hallucinatory process). In order to facilitate the hallucinatory work, many cerebral areas are mobilised (Fox et al., 2013)[10] together with systems of different humoral modulation (Perogamvros & Schwartz, 2012).

It is known that storing images is rather wasteful (it requires much more room than verbal trace storing), however, visual representation is common usage in dreams. We might, therefore, think that the dream "allows itself" figurability every time some functions fail to operate (the executive cortical areas involved in wakefulness and attention that are continuously mobilising); in that way, it can use all the available energy to produce images without creating any imbalance in the system. Yet, the question remains as to the reason for figurability.

Perhaps, without the work of night representation, we would be at the mercy of perceptual fragmentation, which continuously intrudes into our senses. It is not a question of symbolopoiesis, it is a broader concept of mentalization which the creation of the symbol is part of. The dream exercise might be the subjective account of events without any magnifying glass of the frontal acute instances proposed by the eyes of reality. In that sense, the non-REM oneiric thoughts (slow dream waves), which have less vivid and imaginative characteristics than that of the REM sleep, could be preparatory to the REM in that they prepare the scenic display by choosing the details provided by the perceptual traces which will finally flow into the dream. Far from the frontal acute instances, the dream tells the subject's fragmented truth. However, this cannot happen without the advent of the consciousness, which, through the recall of the dream, will sew it together, restoring continuity and intelligibility. Therefore, the dream described during the analytic session is also a hook thrown through the transference in order to catch all that will never be remembered; yet, it acts on the patient's mental activity, determining the lived experiences (symptoms) and writing their history.

In conclusion, and on the basis of these reflections, we could say that the dream is beyond image. There are images that seem to talk to us, others seem as if they are inviting us to listen; there are images that induce us to touch them, but all of them carry a knowledge of the senses which is enlivened only in the dream talking about ourselves.

Notes

1. We can think of dreams as a religion of the mind, in that they furnish a general organisation of the internal world with the function of representing, like a religion, the "sacred things", that is, the internal objects which have assumed theological significance for the individual. (Mancia, 1988, p. 419)

2. Clinical and brain imaging studies link episodic memory and autonoetic awareness with activity in several prefrontal brain regions (medial, dorsolateral), visual cortex, and medial temporal lobe, including the hippocampus. Hippocampal regions are especially implicated when the self-referential quality of the memory task is high. Changes in brain function during REM sleep, especially increased activity in the hippocampal formation and decreased activity in prefrontal regions, are consistent with the view that altered episodic memory functioning linked to these brain regions contributes to the unique quality of dream experience (Nielsen & Stenstrom, 2005, p. 1287).

3. These dreams are available on dreambank.net under the nickname of "Ed". Domhoff uses the Hall Van de Castle code system (1996). He suggested keeping the dream as a kind of "embodied thought". The system's nucleus is based on the idea that the frequency of appearance of an element within a set of dreams reveals the intensity of a concern present in waking life. Alongside this code system, Domhoff adds the "unrealistic element scale" (Domhoff, 1996) for the analysis of bizarre elements in dreams.

4. I think we need first to pay attention to the subjective sense of bizarreness in dreams, and make a distinction between "irrationality" and "bizarreness" in dreams. Most bizarreness is irrational, but not all irrationality is experienced as bizarre. Bizarreness in dreams might be defined as surprising, illogical aspects that engender a feeling of strangeness in the dreamer. Non-bizarre irrationality may objectively look irrational, but it does not engender a feeling of strangeness in the dreamer. (Blechner, 2013, p. 169)

5. Method. Forty-four persons living in the USA who had been recording all their dreams for at least two years were identified through notices placed on websites maintained by the Association of Professional Sleep Societies and the International Association for the Study of Dreams. These forty-four persons sent us twenty dreams each—the last ten dreams they had recorded before 9/11/01 and the first ten dreams recorded after 9/11, without any selection or alteration. Participants included eleven men and thirty-three women, with an age range of twenty-two to seventy years. (Age was not available in a few cases, and, for those available, mean age was forty-eight years.) Participants lived throughout the USA. None lived in Manhattan, and none had relatives or close friends who died in the attack.

6. As defined through the War Stressor Assessment Questionnaire (WSAQ) (Jovic et al., 2002).The two groups gave different answers to the clusters related to passivity (larger number of answers from the experimental group) and those related to activity (larger number of answers from the control group).

7. Psychoanalytic Enunciation Analysis (PEA): this method studies the subject's capacity for symbolising self, objects, and self-object relations represented in the dream. The Moser method: this method includes a process perspective and allows deducting relational capacities (involvement) and the need for security and withdrawal (affect

regulation) of the dreamer on the basis of the manifest dream text. A wide reference to this method can be found in Fonagy et al. (2012).

8. FRED, a Frankfurt group (where FRED stands for Frankfurt fMRI/ EGG depression), has been conducting a study on depressed patients through the analysis of their dreams for many years. The research is being conducted by Sigmund-Freud-Institute (SFI), BIC (the Brain Imaging Centre), with the collaboration of MPIH (Max-Planck-Institute for brain research), all of them located in Frankfurt. The purpose of this study is to examine the changes in cerebral functions of patients with chronic depression who are undergoing therapeutic treatment. The contemplation vertex is the dream that is analysed through the Moser method while the cerebral structures are monitored by fMRI and EEG.

9. First, according to both Freud and Hobson (2013), this state entails a withdrawal of engagement from the external world, but more important—and here too Hobson's new theory agrees with Freud's—it entails deactivation of "the dorsolateral prefrontal cortex (DLPFC), the seat of so-called executive ego mechanisms" (Hobson, in press, p. 38). This deactivation of the executive "ego" has significant consequences for the sleeping mind because "the dorsolateral prefrontal cortex plays a key role in keeping one on track on whatever state of consciousness prevails" (p. 38). Foremost among these consequences is a major reduction in "working memory, self-reflective awareness, volition and planning" (p. 33); that is, a major reduction in what Freud called "secondary process" cognition. This, in turn, releases what Freud called the "primary process" from normal inhibitory constraints. (Solms, 2013, p. 202)

10. As noted by the authors of the original studies, activated regions are highly consistent with the subjective aspects of dreaming. Clusters were observed in numerous high-level visual areas, such as the parahippocampal area, fusiform gyrus, and lingual gyrus, consistent with the ubiquitous, immersive visual imagery characteristic of dreams. Regions implicated in long-term and episodic memory, as well as in imagining future scenes and situations (Schacter & Rose Addis, 2007), are also active, including parahippocampal cortex, hippocampus, and entorhinal cortex. Finally, multiple clusters were observed in mPFC regions, which, most relevant to the present results, have been strongly implicated in self-referential thought and affective decisions (Fox et al., 2013).

References

Alberini, C. M. (2011). The role of reconsolidation and the dynamic process of long-term memory formation and storage. *Frontiers in Behavioral Neuroscience, 5:12* 10.3389/fnbeh.2011.00012.

Alberini, C. M. (2014). Memoria, traccia fragile e dinamica. In: Cena Imbasciati (Ed.), *Neuroscienze e teoria Psicoanalitica*. Milan: Springer.

Balderas, I., Rodriguez-Ortiz, C., & Bermudez-Rattoni, F. (2015). Consolidation and reconsolidation of object recognition memory. *Behavior Brain Research, 15*(285): 213–222.

Blechner, M. J. (2001). *The Dream Frontier*. Hillsdale, NJ: Analytic Press.

Blechner, M. J. (2005). The grammar of irrationality. *Contemporary Psychoanalysis, 41*: 203–221.

Blechner, M. J. (2013). What are dreams like and how does the brain make them that way? *Contemporary Psychoanalysis, 49*(2): 165–175.

Bromberg, P. (2011). *The Shadow of the Tsunami and the Growth of the Relational Mind*. New York: Routledge.

Cartwright, R.,D., Lloyd, S., Knight, S., & Trenholme, I. (1984). Broken dreams: a study of the effects of divorce and depression on dream content. *Psychiatry, 47*(3): 251–259.

Cassirer, E. (1959). *Linguaggio e Mito*. Milan: Il Saggiatore, 1976.

Civitarese, G. (2013). *Il Sogno Necessario. Nuove Teorie e Tecniche dell'Interpretazione in Psicoanalisi*. Milan: Franco Angeli.

Colace, C. (2010). Drug dreams in mescaline and LSD addiction. *American Journal on Addictions, 19*: 192.

Colace, C. (2014). *Drug Dreams: Clinical and Research Implications of Dreams about Drugs in Drug-addicted Patients*. London: Karnac.

Domhoff, W. G. (1996). *Finding Meaning in Dreams: A Quantitative Approach*. New York: Plenum Press.

Domhoff, W. G. (2011). Dreaming as embodied simulation: a widower's dreams of his deceased wife. *Dreaming, 25*(3): 232–256.

Domhoff, W. G., & Fox, C. R. (2015). Dreaming and the default network: a review, synthesis and counterintuitive research proposal. *Consciousness and Cognition, 33*: 342–353.

Ecker, B. (2015). Memory reconsolidation understood and misunderstood. *International Journal of Neuropsychotherapy, 3*(1): 2–46.

Fischmann, T., Russ, M., & Leuzinger-Bohleber, M. (2013). Trauma, dream, and psychic change in psychoanalyses: a dialog between psychoanalysis and the neurosciences. *Frontiers in Human Neuroscience, 7*(87): 1–15.

Fischmann, T., Russ, M., Baehr, T., Stirn, A., & Leuzinger-Bohleber, M. (2012). Changes in dreams of chronic depressed patients: the Frankfurt fMRI/EEG study (FRED). In: P. Fonagy (Ed.), *The Significance of Dreams. Bridging Clinical and Extraclinical Research in Psychoanalysis* (pp. 157–181). London: Karnac.

Fonagy, P., Kachele, H., Leuzinger-Bohleber, M., &Taylor, D. (2012). *The Significance of Dreams*. London: Karnac.

Fosshage, J. (1997). The organizing functions of dream mentation. *Contemporary Psychoanalysis, 33*(3): 429–458.

Fosshage, J. (2013). The dream narrative. *Contemporary Psychoanalysis, 49*(2): 253–258.

Fox, C. R., Nijeboer, S., Solomonova, E., Domhoff, G. W., & Christoff, K. (2013). Dreaming as mind wandering: evidence from functional neuroimaging and first-person content reports. *Frontiers Human Neuroscience, 7*: 412.

Freud, S. (1900a). *The Interpretation of Dreams. S. E., 4–5*. London: Hogarth.

Fromm, E. (1951). *The Forgotten Language: An Introduction to the Understanding of Dreams, Fairy Tales, and Myths*. New York: Rinehart.

Hartmann, E., & Brezler, T. (2008). A systematic change in dreams after 9/11/01. *SLEEP, 31*(2): 213–218.

Hau, S., Jović, V., & Rosenbaum, B. (2013). Traumatic dreams: symbolization and affect regulation. Paper presented to the Prague Panel at the IPA Congress, Prague, 1–3 August.

Hobson, J. A. (2013). Ego ergo sum: toward a psychodynamic neurology. *Contemporary Psychoanalysis, 49*(2): 142–164.

Jović, V., Opacic, G., Knezevic, G., Tenjovic, L., & Lecic-Tosevski, D. (2002). War Stressor Assessment Questionnaire: psychometric evaluation. *Psihijatrija Danas, 34*: 51–75.

Mancia, M. (1988). The dream as religion of the mind. *International Journal of Psychoanalysis, 69*: 419–426.

Mancia, M. (2006). Memoria implicita e inconscio precoce non rimosso: loro ruolo nel transfert e nel sogno. *Rivista di Psicoanalisi, 52*: 629–655.

Nielsen, T. A., & Stenstrom, P. (2005). What are the memory sources of dreaming? *Nature, 437*(7063): 1286–1289.

Nielsen, T. A., Vealain, D. G., Stenstrom, P., & Powel, R. A. (2004). Immediate and delayed incorporations of events into dreams: further replication and implications for dream function. *Journal of Sleep Research, 13*: 327–336.

Paller, K., & Voss, J. (2004). Memory reactivation and consolidation during sleep. *Learning & Memory, 11*: 664–670.

Payne, J., & Nadel, L. (2004). Sleep, dreams, and memory consolidation: the role of the stress hormone cortisol. *Learning & Memory, 11*: 671–678.

Perogamvros, L., & Schwartz, S. (2012). The roles of the reward system in sleep and dreaming. *Neuroscience and Biobehavioral Reviews, 36*: 1934–1951.

Schacter, D. L., & Rose Addis, D. (2007). The cognitive neuroscience of constructive memory: remembering the past and imagining the future. *Philosophical Transactions Royal Society London Biology Science, 362*(1481): 773–786.

Schredl, M. (2010). Characteristics and content in dream. *International Review of Neurobiology, 92*: 135–154.

Solms, M. (2013). Freud's "primary process" versus Hobson's "protoconsciousness". *Contemporary Psychoanalysis, 49*(2): 201–208.

Varvin, S., Fischmann, T., Jović, V., Rosenbaum, B., & Hau, S. (2012). Traumatic dreams: symbolisation gone astray. In: P. Fonagy (Ed.), *The Significance of Dreams. Bridging Clinical and Extraclinical Research in Psychoanalysis* (pp. 182–211). London: Karnac.

Winson, J. (1985). *Brain and Psyche: The Biology of the Unconscious*. Garden City, NY: Anchor Press/Doubleday.

Yovell, Y. (2014). The unconscious and trauma. Paper presented to the Sandler Conference, Frankfurt, 2 March.

Zellner, M. (2013). Dreaming and the default mode network. *Contemporary Psychoanalysis, 49*(2): 226–232.

CHAPTER TWO

Foundations of addiction: dysregulated SEEKING and PANIC processes

Maggie Zellner

Introduction

This chapter gives a very brief overview of a neuropsychoanalytic perspective on addiction (Zellner et al., 2011), which links the cognitive neuroscience findings on addiction with affective neuroscience and psychodynamic concepts. Addiction is such a huge problem that we need to bring all truths to bear on the issue, and certainly each of these fields has discovered some truths about it, although much remains to be fully understood.

This approach to addiction is an excellent exemplar of the broader principle of "dual aspect monism" (Panksepp & Biven, 2012), a perspective taken by many in the neuropsychoanalytic community when trying to explore questions about mental life or psychopathology. This position argues that the brain, which is an object, and the mind, which is the experience of being a subject, are, in fact, two perspectives on the same system. Thus, any question of mental health—even disorders that appear "only" to involve the mind—truly requires us to take both a brain and a mind perspective. Although some have expressed concern about the neuropsychoanalytic enterprise (e.g., Blass & Carmeli, 2007), I believe the intention of neuropsychoanalysis is not to reduce the complex subjective experience of being a person to the objective mechanics of the brain (which actually idealises neuroscience, whose findings are tentative and is in a continual process of development), but to move towards a more complete picture of the phenomenon. In fact, it could also be argued that biological psychiatry and cognitive neuroscience do not consider subjective experience nearly enough, so psychodynamic clinicians and thinkers should be informed so that we can contribute to their dialogue. In addition, because addiction is, at one and the same time, about chemicals that affect the brain and about strong subjective processes that drive behaviour, a neuropsychoanalytic approach that brings brain and mind together is even more clearly relevant.

The phenomenon of addiction, as I shall address it here, involves these key components.

- Craving or compulsion—strong desire for a substance or behaviour that is overwhelming and preoccupying.
- Disregard for negative consequences—the addict knows it is going to end badly but does not care, or rationalises that it will not go badly this time, despite evidence to the contrary.
- Inability to inhibit—cannot regulate the impulse to take the drug or engage in the behaviour.

A mind–brain understanding of addiction, therefore, requires a discussion of the basic features of the mechanisms of "wanting"—both the primary experience of pleasure, and the learning about pleasure—and of the mechanisms of self-control.

This chapter does not provide anything approaching a comprehensive discussion of the current cognitive neuroscience model of addiction; readers can access numerous reviews on the topic (e.g., Volkow et al., 2012, 2016). Evidence is emerging that people can also become addicted to behaviours, such as eating, gambling, internet use, and so on (see, for example, Banz et al., 2016; Gold et al., 2015; Olsen, 2011). In addition, a number of writers have already advanced neuropsychoanalytic perspectives on addiction (see, for example, Johnson, 2011; Johnson et al., 2014; Khantzian, 2003), which should be consulted for a deeper and richer discussion of the topic.

A neuropsychoanalytic perspective

The late Jaak Panksepp, Mark Solms, Doug Watt, and I (Zellner et al., 2011), based on earlier work by Panksepp (e.g., Alcaro & Panksepp, 2011; Panksepp et al., 2002, 2004), have offered a preliminary suggestion of how affective neuroscience and psychoanalytic concepts can shed additional light on the problem of addiction. This neuropsychoanalytic perspective shifts attention to central, internal processes within the person that underlie wellbeing, optimism, and meaning. These processes are fundamentally based in two of the seven "emotion command systems" described by Panksepp (1998): the SEEKING system, which underlies the feeling of interest, expectancy, and motivation and is regulated by dopamine (for an in-depth discussion, see Alcaro & Panksepp, 2011; Wright & Panksepp, 2012; and the chapter on SEEKING in Panksepp & Biven, 2012) and the PANIC/GRIEF system, regulated by opioids, which reduce separation distress and provide a sense of security (see Nelson & Panksepp, 1998; Panksepp, 2003; Stein et al., 2007).

The activity of these two systems, Panksepp argues, underpin whether a person can, on the one hand, find meaning in life and feel interested in natural rewards (mediated by dopamine and related neurotransmitters), and experience a basic sense of security and comfort in his own skin (mediated by opioids), on the other hand. When things have not gone so well, because of early life stress, internal conflicts, and/or genetic vulnerabilities, deficiencies in those systems can leave a person feeling either a deficit in meaning or energy, on the one hand, or a basic sense of discomfort in going-on-being or in relating to others, on the other hand, or both. In these conditions, a person thus becomes vulnerable either to drugs of abuse that affect the dopaminergic and/or opioid systems, or to behaviours which increase dopamine or opioid transmission—fundamentally, because these drugs or behaviours provide either a sense of vitality, interest, and optimism, on the one hand, or comfort and security, on the other hand.

The cognitive neuroscience model of addiction

Dopamine and opioids are also central players in the learning and control mechanisms that have been deeply explored in the cognitive neuroscience of addiction (Volkow et al., 2016). The model is well supported and highly elaborated, summarised succinctly here by Koob and Volkow (2010), two leading researchers in the field:

> Drug addiction is a chronically relapsing disorder that has been characterised by (1) compulsion to seek and take the drug, (2) loss of control in limiting intake, and (3) emergence of a negative emotional state (e.g., dysphoria, anxiety, irritability) reflecting a motivational withdrawal syndrome when access to the drug is prevented. Drug addiction has been conceptualised as a disorder that involves elements of both impulsivity and compulsivity that yield a composite addiction cycle composed of three stages: "binge/intoxication", "withdrawal/ negative affect", and "preoccupation/anticipation" (craving). Animal and human imaging studies have revealed discrete circuits that mediate the three stages of the addiction cycle with key elements of the ventral tegmental area and ventral striatum as a focal point for the binge/intoxication stage, a key role for the extended amygdala in the withdrawal/negative affect stage, and an important role in the preoccupation/anticipation stage for a widely distributed network involving the orbitofrontal cortex–dorsal striatum, prefrontal cortex, basolateral amygdala, hippocampus, and insula involved in craving, and the cingulate gyrus, dorsolateral prefrontal, and inferior frontal cortices in disrupted inhibitory control. The transition to addiction involves neuroplasticity in all of these structures that can begin with changes in the mesolimbic dopamine system and a cascade of neuroadaptations from the ventral striatum to the dorsal striatum and orbitofrontal cortex and, eventually, dysregulation of the prefrontal cortex, cingulate gyrus, and extended amygdala. (p. 217)

There are several stages in the cognitive neuroscience model. First, there is a subjective experience associated with a particular drug, depending on its mechanism of action (for example, energy and euphoria with cocaine or amphetamine, due to dopamine transmission; disinhibition with alcohol via enhanced GABA transmission; or warmth and relaxation with opiates, via *mu*-opioid stimulation (see Hyman et al., 2006, for review). Then, because all drugs of abuse lead to increased dopamine in the nucleus accumbens (NAcc) (Volkow et al., 2007), the actions leading to drug taking are reinforced (Everitt & Robbins, 2005) (even if increased dopamine is not central in the acute subjective effect of the drug, like nicotine), and the cues associated with those experiences acquire "enhanced motivational value of the drug, secondary to learned associations through conditioning and habits" (Volkow et al., 2007). This "incentive salience" (Berridge & Robinson, 1998) shifts the person's attention to getting more of the drug or participating more in the behaviour. Additionally, craving for the drug or behaviour can be stimulated by cues associated with it. In tandem, the appeal of natural rewards is diminished. Finally, following extended use, the ability of the person to inhibit behaviour is impaired, due to the effects on prefrontal cortical circuits associated with behaviour regulation.

As indicated above, I am dramatically oversimplifying a much more nuanced and complicated model, and the reader is encouraged to learn more about it in the cited reviews. However, it is reasonable to say that one of the core mechanisms described in the cognitive neuroscience model of addiction is that drugs of abuse directly stimulate the circuits that facilitate learning about what we want, so we begin to want the drugs and the cues associated with the drugs (or behaviours).

In most research involving addiction, reward processes, basic pleasure and aversion, and reward-learning, and behavioural regulation, the following brain regions are centrally involved:

- brain stem: triggering primary emotion patterns, including the periaqueductal grey (PAG), which mediates core feelings of aversion or wellbeing;
- hypothalamus: monitoring need states, sensitising responses to environment and energising seeking behaviour and/or effortful activity for particular rewards;
- amygdala: learning about cues associated with outcomes;
- ventral striatum: energising motivation and SEEKING;
- dorsal striatum: procedural learning and habit acquisition;
- orbitofrontal cortex (OFC): relative value of rewards;
- anterior insula: affective meaning;
- anterior cingulate: conflict monitoring, behavioural switching;
- prefrontal cortex: regulating affect and behaviour.

The circuits that regulate emotion are more ventral; those that are involved with guiding attention voluntarily are more dorsal. These areas are some of the last circuits to mature and they are highly influenced by our experience, especially in our families.

Addictive processes and everyday experience

From a neuropsychoanalytic point of view, addiction is a distortion or dysregulation of fundamental processes we all share, having to do with wellbeing, wanting, learning, motivation, and self-control. As mammals, our evolutionary heritage provides us with the mechanisms to experience pleasure related to having our needs satisfied, and to learn about what to do again to achieve future satisfactions. Also, we become attached to, and feel pleasure with, the people who keep us safe and provide us with companionship and resources. The brain mechanisms underlying all these processes are recruited in addiction, but the mechanisms themselves are vital for our survival.

Therefore, as I put addiction into an affective neuroscience context, I want to emphasise that anyone who is not an addict already experiences, in everyday life, all of the basic components that are recruited in a magnified, or dysregulated way, in addicts. We have the capacity to feel pleasure or other positive consequences of our actions. We know what it is like to want those things again, to feel craving, and to feel motivated to take actions to fulfil our desires. We also know what it is like to want things that are not good for us, and almost everyone has had the experience of doing something we know will have a bad outcome, no matter how trivial, such as eating too much ice cream when trying to lose weight, or staying up late when we know we will feel tired tomorrow.

However, if we are not addicts, we can take pleasure in rather ordinary things, and we do not require high levels of novelty; we are generally able to do things with negative consequences in moderation, and, perhaps most importantly, we have the capacity refrain from, or inhibit, an action if we imagine strongly negative future consequences. For an addict, however, most, or all, of these processes tend to be dysregulated.

The affective neuroscience context for a neuropsychoanalytic hypothesis of addiction

First, I shall briefly summarise the emotion command systems, and then focus on the ones that might be central to addiction. For details, see Panksepp and Biven (2012).

- The SEEKING system: fundamentally the dopaminergic pathway that goes from the ventral tegmental area (VTA) at the top of the brain stem, projecting to the nucleus accumbens, amygdala, and up into the ventral forebrain. We need to go out in the world and get all of the good things in life that are out there, and learn about the actions that get our needs met and the objects and contexts associated with them. Activity in the SEEKING system underlies much of this: first, there is the feeling of being interested, enthusiastic, motivated, optimistic, then there is learning about things and situations so we can pursue them again. Dopamine facilitates both aspects of SEEKING. The best illustration is the magnified activity of this system when affected by drugs that increase the production or persistence of dopamine, like cocaine or amphetamine—a person becomes super enthusiastic and interested, talkative, full of ideas. DA is released when we encounter novelty, and when we consume rewards, but as we learn about cues, the DA release shifts from consumption to the cues that predict the drugs. This is related to the positive affect when expecting a reward, like the rats that chirp when put back in the context where they were tickled; rats also emit these chirps when they have acquired a cocaine habit and they are put in a box with the cocaine lever (Burgdorf & Panksepp, 2006).
- RAGE: defensive behaviour, designed to confront competitors or fight off an attacker.
- FEAR: designed to help to detect and run away from things that might cause physical injury or death.
- LUST: sexual behaviours. Sex feels good, of course, and is associated with increased dopamine and opioids.
- CARE: the instinct to respond to others, particularly babies and children, when they are in distress.
- SEPARATION DISTRESS, which also is called the PANIC system, underlies the behaviour and affect triggered by separation, similar to the attachment–loss system described by Bowlby (1969): arousal, searching, and crying in initial response to separation (accompanied by increased stress hormones, norepinephrine, and dopamine), and the despair phase following loss, which involves quieting and reduced dopamine transmission, together with a drop in opioids. Separation distress is profoundly reduced by opioids.

- PLAY: an instinct for engaging in creative exploratory activity that is not designed for a specific goal, but often involves practising for adult behaviours.

The core of addiction is based on fundamentally healthy processes that are critical to our survival, which have become deranged or out of balance. Our brains are "pre-wired" to learn about things that feel good, seek them out again, to feel motivated to exert effort to get them, to focus on the cues and situations that are associated with them, and to feel that something is missing when we are experiencing an absence.

The neuropsychoanalytic perspective, as mentioned, focuses on the SEEKING and PANIC systems as central players in addiction because of the affects involved. First, it feels positive to feel interested, expectant, hopeful, energised—this is largely mediated by the dopaminergic SEEKING system. The seeking experience is, "I want something that's going to happen in the future; I am going somewhere to get something that I want or need." Second, the affect produced by opioid transmission, in contrast, which modulates attachment and the PANIC system, is comfort, satiation, soothing, relaxation. This is the affect I argue is properly called "pleasure"—a delicious meal, a hug, a massage, an orgasm: a consummatory experience. The experience of pleasure is, "I like this moment. I want to stay here right now." Opioids also generate a feeling of safety or security.

Not surprisingly, there is a deep correspondence between attachment and drug addiction, especially opiate addiction, as Insel (2003) has pointed out, as well as Panksepp (1998). Many of the feelings and behaviours of opiate withdrawal—restlessness, unease, crying, aches, anguish—are very similar to the feelings of heartbreak and loss. From an affective neuroscience perspective, it makes perfect sense that these phenomena overlap. The panic system evolved in order to foster social bonds; good opioid levels are the indication that we are close to those we care about and are safe. This means that we stay close to those we care about; we protect each other, and co-operate to get resources, helping us to succeed as a species. The price we pay for this evolutionary advantage is the pain of social loss (Panksepp, 2005). This, I think, is really the most significant motivator for most humans: we are afraid of loss or separation distress. So, the flip side of the pleasures of closeness is the benefit of avoiding such pain. Neurochemically speaking, we cling to each other in order to keep our μ-opioid receptor activity contentedly high and to prevent them from dropping distressingly low (Panksepp, 1998).

Thus, ideally, if your baseline SEEKING system activity is healthy, you find life generally meaningful, and you often have energy to exert effort towards goals, you have things to look forward to, you can enjoy learning. You have the ability to explore and to play. Similarly, in an ideal situation, if your baseline opioid levels are optimal, you feel relatively secure, and relatively comfortable in your own skin.

However, you might not be so lucky, and here is the heart of this neuropsychoanalytic hypothesis about addiction. If, because of genetic differences, early life stress, current life stress, or psychodynamic conflicts, or some combination of these, your SEEKING system is underactive, you might feel a chronic deficit in enthusiasm or motivation, interest or meaning. If your baseline opioid levels are low, you might feel chronic low self-esteem, unease, not being comfortable in your own skin. If this is the case, you might, therefore, be vulnerable to responding strongly to drugs or behaviours that stimulate SEEKING, because that helps you have a feeling of optimism, agency, and motivation. Or you might respond to opiates, or behaviours that increase opioids, to generate a feeling of security or attachment.

In other words, people might be vulnerable to addiction because the systems that underlie wellbeing, which are recruited by drugs of abuse or addictive behaviour, are already impaired. There is strong evidence that addicts have variations in dopamine receptors (Volkow et al., 2012) but it is not clear to what extent this precedes, or is a result of, the acquisition of addiction. Addicts often report feeling normal for the first time when they first get high or drink alcohol. Certainly, some may acquire deficiencies in these systems subsequent to long-term drug use, which alters the level of receptors, or neurotransmitter production or transporters, or other regulatory aspects of these systems. In these cases, the "gas" of the system drives addiction; the craving for the drugs or behaviours that substitute for what is missing under normal circumstances.

It might also be that if a person with genetic or historical vulnerability is offered drugs, they might have less motivation to put the brakes on themselves, because they are not as invested in avoiding long-term negative consequences. A healthy person, when offered something like cocaine, whether as a novice or as someone who knows that trouble ensues from getting high, might be able to choose between the two rewards, cocaine and a healthy lifestyle. However, if a person has a genetic vulnerability, or grew up with an alcoholic, narcissistic, depressed, abusive, or neglectful parent, let us say, and did not get enough developmental needs met, they might think: "I know cocaine is probably addictive (or, I get crazy when I get high), but for me right now it is so much more important to feel good today, I don't care what happens tomorrow, much less a year from now."

In addition, there is a question of putting the brakes on a behaviour simply because we have had enough for the moment. In the normal, healthy organism, there is a flexibility and frequent oscillation between the states of SEEKING and pleasure, between appetite and consummation, between "wanting" and "liking" (Berridge & Kringelbach, 2008); we are always a little bit in the state of desire and we are having lots of little moments of consummation. In healthy people, these systems are active most of the time, to a greater or lesser degree, because even if one need is met (such as being hungry), another soon arises (needing company, for example). All things being equal, when you have met a need, there is a satisfaction signal, which terminates the behaviour, so you can move on to meeting other needs, sensing other desires.

Thus, another problem with addiction is that the appetitive–consummatory fluctuation might be distorted or imbalanced, or overly focused on one "reward" among many. For example, a person can take a drug that stimulates the SEEKING system to a large extent, such as cocaine, but never produces a consummatory pleasure. It is hard to imagine a person saying, "Mmm, that was a really good cocaine high, I think I've had enough for now." For most addicts, there is never really a feeling of being satiated, and feeling interested in moving on to other rewards, even for behaviours in which there is a strongly designed satiation signal, such as for eating and sex. In Alcoholics Anonymous, they say, "One is too many and a thousand never enough." That is the essence of addiction: I want, I want more, and I want it now, and no matter how much of it I get, I need more.

In conclusion, our neuropsychoanalytic hypothesis is that what addicts really want (Zellner et al., 2011) is to feel that core sense of enthusiasm in the world, a sense of being an effective agent in a world filled with meaning, with the energy to stay focused on goals and get things done, and to have a sense of hope and optimism about the future. Alternatively, or perhaps in conjunction, addicts are trying to soothe a sense of loneliness or insecurity, a chronic low level of well-being. Furthermore, addicts in the long run develop an attachment to, or a relationship with, the substance that can then stand in for, or occupy the space of, relationships with people. In fact, one of the "benefits" of addictive substances and behaviours is that they are under the addict's control, and their effects are predictable, as opposed to emotional relationships and the vagaries of other people. In this respect, then, it is possible that Insel's link between addiction and attachment went in the wrong direction—it is not that attachment is a form of addiction, but, rather, addiction makes use of, or is a distortion of, the healthy processes of attachment and can even be an attempt to take its place.

Enriching or perhaps reorientating the cognitive neuroscience model of addiction

A neuropsychoanalytic hypothesis of addiction does not seek to deny or replace the findings on the powerful learning that takes place during intoxication ("incentive salience") and the effects of long-term use on the capacity for self-control, because, clearly, those processes are important, and because intrinsic satisfaction from natural rewards becomes further degraded as the SEEKING circuitry becomes hijacked by drugs of abuse. For an addicted person, the rest of the world seems very grey and boring. The things that used to bring pleasure do not any more, which makes the drug, gambling, shopping, compulsive sex, or other things more and more necessary because everything is getting flatter and washed out in the world.

However, because cognitive neuroscience research has focused on the learning element, and the extent to which cues and context can reinstate addictive behaviour, it is easy to come away from that literature thinking that almost anyone can acquire an addiction simply due to the effects of the drugs on the circuits mediating learning. Also, the neuroscience research to date puts perhaps too much emphasis on external factors—the cues associated with addiction, which trigger craving—and not enough on the internal factors which make a person vulnerable to craving, or impaired in taking care of themselves by choosing long-term wellbeing over short-term gratification. The neuropsychoanalytic prediction is that if a person can feel more intrinsic meaning and motivation in life (probably mediate by good baseline dopamine activity), and feels relatively comfortable in her skin (probably mediated by good baseline opioid tone), then the cues associated with drugs or compulsive behaviour would lose their "pull". In fact, this is consistent with the interesting fact that the acquisition of addictive behaviour is largely tested on stressed and lonely animals. Rats are social animals that like to run around and explore, and most of our research is done on rats that are living in little boxes and have very little opportunity for play. They are stressed and have very little stimulation. The evidence is that when they have other rewards present, animals are much less likely to acquire addictions, and are less vulnerable to relapse ("reinstatement") (Puhl et al., 2012; Ranaldi et al., 2011).

In contrast to the model that emphasises learning, habit, and external cues, then (which portrays an addict as living in world of things "stamped" with salience and drawn like robots to the things and behaviours associated with dopamine and opioid transmission), what we are proposing is that an internal source is the primary mechanism of addiction, which is then strongly influenced by learning. Thus, a neuropsychoanalytic perspective places the subject at the centre of the addictive process, rather than the cues in the environment (although those are important as well).

Conclusion:
some brief comments on treatment implications

A sufficient discussion of treatment is beyond the scope of this chapter, but I offer a few tentative thoughts in that direction. One implication of the ideas raised by a neuropsychoanalytic hypothesis about addiction is that we can work with our patients to recognise how much they have a relationship with that drug or with that behaviour. Not only are they trying to use their addiction in order to not feel lonely in the world, but giving up that thing can also make them feel lonely because that is an attachment as well. Some tolerance of loss and separation distress, some grieving, might be part of achieving abstinence.

Psychotherapy should also work to address the internal causes of low self-esteem; one aspect of this, psychodynamically speaking, might be our conflicted attachments to negative internal objects. Addiction could simultaneously be an effort to soothe loneliness, complying with a sadistic other by damaging the self, or attacking the other by sabotaging one's own life through addiction. In addition, community social support is also vital, and psychotherapy can help support a person to engage more in other supports, like 12-Step programmes or other community activities, as well as to take more risks in life towards connection and fulfilment, or to face fears involved with taking risks to address external difficulties. Moreover, this perspective, based in affective neurosciences, highlights the need for societies to address significant external stressors such as intergenerational trauma and poverty, or oppressive life circumstances, which exert huge stresses on people, and makes them vulnerable to drugs or behaviours which temporarily induce positive affect.

We can also use neuroscience to offer hypotheses to patients, or education to support their sobriety. It might help a patient to know that drugs have affected their ability to control themselves, or to feel that life is worth living without them, because their brain circuits have been affected. It might help addicts to remain abstinent if they learn that there is some capacity for the system to re-equilibrate, or come back to a healthier level, such as methamphetamine users whose level of D2 receptor return to normal levels after a year of abstinence (Volkow et al., 2012), and prefrontal cortex changes with abstinence (Garavan et al., 2013). This is also reflected in the practice in Alcoholics Anonymous to count days and announce anniversaries; abstinence is supported by a realisation that the more time between you and a substance, the better chance at health you have.

These are just some brief offerings to the psychotherapist about how these ideas can be used to support treatment. I hope, at a minimum, this chapter has helped those who are new to neuroscience to productively engage with the emerging literature on addiction, and, thereby, add psychodynamic perspectives to the dialogue. Much remains to be explored, but the possibility of achieving deep understanding, and truly effective treatment, might be at hand in this new era of integrating brain and mind perspectives.

References

Alcaro, A., & Panksepp, J. (2011). The SEEKING mind: primal neuro-affective substrates for appetitive incentive states and their pathological dynamics in addictions and depression. *Neuroscience Biobehavioral Reviews, 35*(9): 1805–1820.

Banz, B. C., Yip, S. W., Yau, Y. H. C., & Potenza, M. N. (2016). Behavioral addictions in addiction medicine: from mechanisms to practical considerations. *Progress in Brain Research, 223*: 311–328.

Berridge, K. C., & Kringelbach, M. L. (2008). Affective neuroscience of pleasure: reward in humans and animals. *Psychopharmacology, 199*: 457–480.

Berridge, K. C., & Robinson, T. E. (1998). What is the role of dopamine in reward: hedonic impact, reward learning, or incentive salience? *Brain Research Reviews, 28*: 309–369.

Blass, R. B., & Carmeli, Z. (2007). The case against neuropsychoanalysis. On fallacies underlying psychoanalysis' latest scientific trend and its negative impact on psychoanalytic discourse. *International Journal of Psychoanalysis, 88*: 19–40.

Bowlby, J. (1969). *Attachment and Loss. Volume 1.* New York: Basic Books.

Burgdorf, J., & Panksepp, J. (2006). The neurobiology of positive emotions. *Neuroscience and Biobehavioral Reviews, 30*(2): 173–187.

Everitt, B. J., & Robbins, T. W. (2005). Neural systems of reinforcement for drug addiction: from actions to habits to compulsion. *Nature Neuroscience, 8*: 1481–1489.

Garavan, H., Brennan, K., Hester, R., & Whelan, R. (2013). The neurobiology of successful abstinence. *Current Opinion in Neurobiology, 23*(4): 668–674.

Gold, M. S., Badgaiyan, R. D., & Blum, K. (2015). A shared molecular and genetic basis for food and drug addiction: overcoming hypodopaminergic trait/state by incorporating dopamine agonistic therapy in psychiatry. *The Psychiatric Clinics of North America, 38*(3): 419–462. doi: 10.1016/j.psc.2015.05.011

Hyman, S. E., Malenka, R. C., & Nestler, E. J. (2006). Neural mechanisms of addiction: the role of reward-related learning and memory. *Annual Review of Neuroscience, 29*: 565–598.

Insel, T. R. (2003). Is social attachment an addictive disorder? *Physiology & Behavior, 79*(3): 351–357.

Johnson, B. (2011). Psychoanalytic treatment of psychological addiction to alcohol (alcohol abuse). *Frontiers in Psychology, 2*: 362. doi: 10.3389/fpsyg.2011.00362.

Johnson, B., Ulberg, S., Shivale, S., Donaldson, J., Milczarski, B., & Faraone, S. V. (2014). Fibromyalgia, autism, and opioid addiction as natural and induced disorders of the endogenous opioid hormonal system. *Discovery Medicine*, *18*(99): 209–220.

Khantzian, E. J. (2003). Understanding addictive vulnerability: an evolving psychodynamic perspective. *Neuropsychoanalysis*, *5*(1): 5–21.

Koob, G. F., & Volkow, N. D. (2010). Neurocircuitry of addiction. *Neuropsychopharmacology*, *35*(1): 217–238.

Nelson, E. E., & Panksepp, J. (1998). Brain substrates of infant–mother attachment: contributions of opioids, oxytocin, and norepinephrine. *Neuroscience and Biobehavioral Reviews*, *22*(3): 437–452.

Olsen, C. M. (2011). Natural rewards, neuroplasticity, and non-drug addictions. *Neuropharmacology*, *61*(7): 1109–1122.

Panksepp, J. (1998). *Affective Neuroscience: The Foundations of Human and Animal Emotions*. New York: Oxford University Press.

Panksepp, J. (2003). Neuroscience. Feeling the pain of social loss. *Science*, *302*(5643): 237–239.

Panksepp, J. (2005). Why does separation distress hurt? Comment on MacDonald and Leary (2005). *Psychological Bulletin*, *131*(2): 224–230; author reply 237–240.

Panksepp, J., & Biven, L. (2012). *The Archaeology of Mind: Neuroevolutionary Origins of Human Emotions*. New York: Norton.

Panksepp, J., Knutson, B., & Burgdorf, J. (2002). The role of brain emotional systems in addictions: a neuro-evolutionary perspective and new "self-report" animal model. *Addiction*, *97*(4): 459–469.

Panksepp, J., Nocjar, C., Burgdorf, J., & Huber, R. (2004). The role of emotional systems in addiction: a neuroethological perspective. *Nebraska Symposium on Motivation*, *50*: 85–126.

Puhl, M. D., Blum, J. S., Acosta-Torres, S., & Grigson, P. S. (2012). Environmental enrichment protects against the acquisition of cocaine self-administration in adult male rats, but does not eliminate avoidance of a drug-associated saccharin cue. *Behavioural Pharmacology*, *23*(1): 43–53. doi: 10.1097/FBP.0b013e32834eb060.

Ranaldi, R., Kest, K., Zellner, M., & Hachimine-Semprebom, P. (2011). Environmental enrichment administered after establishment of cocaine self-administration reduces lever pressing in extinction and during a cocaine context renewal test. *Behavioural Pharmacology*, *22*: 347–353.

Stein, D. J., Van Honk, J., Ipser, J., Solms, M., & Panksepp, J. (2007). Opioids: from physical pain to the pain of social isolation. *CNS Spectrums*, *12*(9): 669–674.

Volkow, N. D., Fowler, J. S., Wang, G. J., Swanson, J. M., & Telang, F. (2007). Dopamine in drug abuse and addiction: results of imaging studies and treatment implications. *Archives of Neurology, 64*(11): 1575–1579.

Volkow, N. D., Koob, G. F., & McLellan, A. T. (2016). Neurobiologic advances from the brain disease model of addiction. *New England Journal of Medicine, 374*(4): 363–371.

Volkow, N. D., Wang, G. J., Fowler, J. S., & Tomasi, D. (2012). Addiction circuitry in the human brain. *Annual Review of Pharmacology and Toxicology, 52*: 321–336.

Wright, J. S., & Panksepp, J. (2012). An evolutionary framework to understand foraging, wanting, and desire: the neuropsychology of the SEEKING system. *Neuropsychoanalysis, 4*(1): 5–39.

Zellner, M. R., Watt, D. F., Solms, M., & Panksepp, J. (2011). Affective neuroscientific and neuropsychoanalytic approaches to two intractable psychiatric problems: why depression feels so bad and what addicts really want. *Neuroscience and Biobehavioral Reviews, 35*(9): 2000–2008.

CHAPTER THREE

Depression in neuropsychoanalysis: why does depression feel bad?

Mark Solms

Introduction

Sometimes, it is necessary to review the basics in order to see the big picture, and there are some very basic things that I would like to review in this chapter. Reading the subtitle of my chapter, which is based on earlier papers (Solms & Panksepp, 2010; Watt & Panksepp, 2009; Zellner et al., 2011), readers might think I am asking a silly question. However, this is a question that we really do need to ask, because, in psychiatry today, it is a question that is not even considered. *Why* the patient feels what he is feeling, what the feeling *means* (psychologically), and what the feeling *does* (causally), are not serious questions in contemporary psychiatry.

In psychoanalysis, we believe that feelings exist for a reason (Solms, in press). They are not epiphenomena; they are not something that is just "nice to have", added on to the brain's *real* workings. Feelings are absolutely central to how the brain works. If we do not take account of feelings, we will never understand the brain. Sentience is *the* distinguishing property of the brain; it is what sets it apart from all other organs. This is what Freud thought. However, in academic psychology and psychiatry through the twentieth century, other ideas took hold. Now, in the twenty-first century, we in neuropsychoanalysis want to return to Freud's original idea, taking account of what has been learnt by other mental science disciplines in the intervening century. That is why we must consider such simple questions afresh.

Let us take an extremely basic example. If you meet a friend and she looks sad, that means something. It tells you something about what is going on inside her, and it gives you an indication as to how she might respond to you (i.e., it has causal implications). She will behave differently if she is sad from how she might behave if she were angry or anxious. This is because different feelings *mean* different things, and they make people *do* different things. Nothing could be more obvious. Right?

Well, let us see what the experts think . . .

Behaviourism

This was the approach to the mind that replaced psychoanalysis in the academic psychology of the mid twentieth century. Freud (1940a) wrote that conscious feeling was "the most unique characteristic" of the part of nature that we call the mind—"a fact without parallel". He then added,". . . one extreme line of thought, exemplified in the American doctrine of behaviourism, thinks it possible to construct a psychology which disregards this fundamental fact!" (Freud, 1940a, p. 157).

It is well known why behaviourists wanted to construct a science of the mind that disregarded its most unique characteristic. Consciousness cannot be observed externally; it is not amenable to *objective* scrutiny. Consciousness is, for that reason, an embarrassment to science, the ideal of which is objective fact over subjective experience. The behaviourists, who wanted to treat the mind as if it were no different from any other part of nature, therefore ruled subjectivity out of court, and limited scientific psychology to the study of the externally observable *outputs* of the mind—to the study of *behaviour*. Objective experimental manipulations ("stimuli") could then be used to discover the causal mechanisms of behavioural "responses". In this way, the intervening variables (conceptualised as *learning*) became the only valid objects of psychological science.

Not surprisingly, a school of thought predicated on the assumption that the mind consists in nothing but learning (e.g., depression is a learnt response), and disregards all the mental phenomena that we "know immediately and from our most personal experience" (Freud, 1940a), was doomed to failure. To deny the causal influence on behaviour of conscious states (like feelings) is to deny the obvious. If one says, that person committed suicide because he could not stand the pain any longer, one is describing the simple causal power of the unfortunate person's feelings. If one were to try to reframe such causal relations so as to exclude the feelings, and base them on learning alone, one would be doing obvious violence to the actual scientific facts.

Cognitive science

Thankfully, therefore, in the last quarter of the twentieth century, realism triumphed over fundamentalism, and feelings found their way back into psychological science. Even though consciousness still cannot be observed directly, or objectively, cognitive scientists today are, nevertheless, willing to acknowledge its existence in their experimental subjects, and, on this basis, to infer the causal mechanisms by which conscious states influence behaviours—in much the same way as the behaviourists were willing to infer the causal mechanisms of learning.

Or are they?

The mechanisms of consciousness may be ontologically equivalent to those of learning (or anything else in the mind) but the *mechanisms* of consciousness differ in fundamental respects from consciousness *itself*. Mechanisms of all kinds are abstractions, *inferred* from experience;[1] they are not experiences themselves. The mechanisms of consciousness, like all other mechanisms, therefore present no special problems for science; they, too, can be described from an objective standpoint, from the third-person point of view, as *functions*. But this excludes the 'fundamental fact' of felt consciousness, namely that we experience it directly.

Is consciousness not perhaps still an embarrassment to science: do cognitive scientists today not perhaps still think it possible to construct a psychology which disregards the *causal* role of feelings—this uniquely subjective characteristic of the mind—the fundamental characteristic of this part of nature?

Cognitive neuroscience

It is, in my view, no accident that the apparent readmittance of consciousness to psychology coincided with advances in the neurosciences which made it possible to study the physiological correlates of almost any mental state. By shifting the focus of their research efforts to the physical correlates of consciousness, neuroscientists were able to pay lip service to its existence without having to trouble themselves too much with its intrinsically subjective nature—with the original source of the embarrassment.

Small wonder, then, that so many behaviourists made such a seamless transition to the new paradigm. As Freud (1940a) put it,

> There would thus be no alternative left to assuming that there are physical or somatic processes which are concomitant with the psychical ones and which we should necessarily have to recognize as more complete than the psychical sequences . . . [Then] it of course becomes plausible to lay the stress in psychology on those somatic processes, to see in *them* the true essence of what is psychical. (p. 157)

To seek the essence of what is psychical in something which lacks its most unique property is surely to look in the wrong place. However, this does not mean that we must abandon reality. Neither does it mean (today) that the brain is the wrong place to seek an understanding of consciousness. It means only that we must admit that consciousness actually exists, that it is a property of nature, that it is a property of the part of nature called the brain, and that this property is no less real and no less causally efficacious than any other natural properties. This, in turn, means that we must recognise that the brain is not quite the same as every other part of nature. The brain has some special properties, and central among these is feeling. As a consequence of it being conscious, the brain behaves differently from most other things, even from other bodily organs.

As far as I can tell, despite appearances, these views are still not generally accepted, or at least they are not generally incorporated into the current theoretical paradigms of cognitive neuroscience. In fact, the very power of cognitive neuroscience seems to be that it treats the organ of the mind as if it were no different from any other bodily organ, indeed from any other complex mechanism—living or dead.

As Oliver Sacks put it,

> Neuropsychology, like classical neurology, aims to be entirely objective, and its great power, its advances, come from just this. But a living creature, and especially a human being, is first and last active – a subject, not an object. It is precisely the subject, the living "I", which is being excluded. Neuropsychology is admirable, but it excludes the psyche – it excludes the experiencing, active, living "I". (Sacks, 1984, p. 164)

Biological psychiatry

The baneful consequences of this continued neglect of the fundamental fact of consciousness have been even more evident in the field of biological psychiatry than in cognitive neuroscience. This is perhaps not surprising, because psychiatry is all about feelings. How else does it differ from neurology?

In biological psychiatry today, if one says, the patient committed suicide because he could not stand the pain any longer, one seems to mean, the patient *thought* he was committing suicide because he could not stand the pain any longer, but *really* he was committing suicide because his serotonin levels were depleted (or something like that). The point is, what the patient says, thinks, or feels may be left out of the scientific account; feelings evidently are not part of the actual causal chain of events. They are just a layperson's translation of the real state of affairs in the brain. This is just fundamentalism.

Depression in biological psychiatry

I shall now illustrate this problem in modern psychiatry with reference to our particular question: why depression feels bad.

As I have said, this question is not even posed in biological psychiatry. It is not posed because what depression feels like does not matter in contemporary psychiatric science. This is evidently because feelings in general do not matter. What matters in biological psychiatry, no less than cognitive neuroscience, are the physical correlates of the feelings. This approach is based on a serious misconception of how the brain works, which will almost inevitably lead to grave mistakes. In their haste to avoid the embarrassingly subjective phenomena of depression, psychiatric researchers have, in recent decades, focused on all sorts of things that correlate with depression, or facilitate it, or contextualise it, and the neural mechanisms of those things, rather than depression itself.

The main focus of depression research for the past few decades has been the neurophysiological mechanisms of serotonin depletion (Harro & Oreland, 2001; Schildkraut, 1965), including the neurotrophic effects of this depletion (Koziek et al., 2008), the neuroendocrinological mechanisms of stress (which has similar neurotrophic consequences (De Kloet et al., 2005)), the neuro-immunological equivalents of these mechanisms (McEwen, 2007), their interactions with sleep mechanisms (Zupancic & Guilleminault, 2006), their genetic underpinnings (Levinson, 2006), and so on. These research programmes have evidently been followed because the mechanisms of serotonin depletion (and its cognates) are eminently tractable scientific problems—notwithstanding the fact that they have nothing to do with actually researching depressive feelings.

The reason these programmes have been followed cannot possibly be because the researchers concerned seriously thought that depressive feelings (let alone major depression) are actually caused by low levels of serotonin. There is not a shred of evidence for that. In fact, it is well established that experimental depletion of brain serotonin does not cause depression (Delgado et al., 1990). Neither was there ever any reason to believe that serotonin would play any such specific causal role in depressive mood. Serotonin is a general purpose modulator of moods and emotions, not only of depressive ones (Berger et al., 2009). It is probably for this reason that SSRIs are used to treat not only depression, but also a host of other emotional troubles, such as panic attacks and obsessive compulsive disorder. This is also probably the reason why SSRIs do not work in so many cases of depression, and why they work only partially or temporarily in the vast majority of cases (cf. STAR*D findings). The same applies to the various cascades associated with serotonin depletion: stress, or inflammation, or hippocampal shrinkage. None of these things has a specific causal relationship with depression. They are too general, "too much" of an explanation. Their main attraction is only that they are scientifically tractable and, therefore, scientifically respectable, objective mechanisms.

In summary, it is clear that, although the mechanisms of serotonin depletion and its cognates correlate with, or facilitate or contextualise, depression, something else—something far more specific—must be the actual causal mechanism of depression. I suggest that this "something else" most likely has to do with the brain mechanisms that actually generate depressive *feelings*.

Depression itself

My reason for suggesting this is the fact that the clinical *phenomenology* of depression is characterised, above all else, by a complex of feelings: low mood, low self-esteem, loss of motivation and energy, guilt, loss of pleasure in the world, and so on. Is this complex of feelings not the most obvious place to seek the essential nature of depression? And dare we ask whether this constellation of feelings means anything? It is, after all, in the essential nature of feelings that they mean something. It would be entirely normal and reasonable for all of us (even we scientists) to ask—outside of our scientific work—what it might mean when somebody says that they feel down, bad, defeated, useless, that they have lost all hope for themselves, lost all interest in other people, and so on. We would ask, *why* do they feel this? Certainly, it is possible that the feelings are meaningless epiphenomena of depression—even though feelings are not normally meaningless—but it is at least equally possible (and in my view, more so) that they are not meaningless.

I think the most helpful way of making sense of this complex of feelings is suggested by what the *DSM IV* definition of major depression described as diagnostic criterion E: "The symptoms are not better accounted for by *bereavement*" (my emphasis).

This differential diagnostic criterion suggests that depression can be easily mistaken for bereavement, which, in turn, suggests that depression is characterised by a complex of feelings that closely resembles those associated with grief. Therefore, it seems reasonable to infer that depression might have something to do with social *loss*.

This reminds us of what the early psychological investigators of depression (who were not embarrassed by feelings and their meanings) concluded on the basis of talking to patients about what their depression might mean to them personally: they concluded that depression was akin to *grief*, that it seemed, in fact, to be a pathological form of *mourning* (Freud, 1917e).[2]

It is, in fact, well established today that early separation experiences do indeed predispose to depression (Heim & Nemeroff, 1999; Pryce et al., 2005), possibly through mediation of the stress cascades that McEwan (2000) has identified, and possibly also via other "general sickness" mechanisms (McEwen, 2007). We also know that a first depressive episode is most likely to be triggered by social loss (Bowlby, 1980), and so on.

Affective neuroscience

In the light of such commonplace observations to the effect that depressive feelings are connected with the psychology of attachment and loss, why are cognitive neuroscientists not focusing their attention on the mammalian brain systems that evolved specifically for the purpose of mediating attachment and loss, and which produce the particular type of pain associated with these biological phenomena of universal significance, that is, separation distress (also known as "protest" or "panic") which, if it does not result in reunion, is typically followed by hopeless "despair"?

It is well established that a specific mammalian brain system evolved precisely to generate these depression-like feelings (Panksepp, 1998, 2003a,b, 2005). This brain system evolved from general pain mechanisms, millions of years ago, apparently for the purpose of forging long-term attachments between mothers and their offspring, between sexual mates, and, ultimately, between social groups in general. When such social bonds are broken through separation or loss of a loved one, or the like, then these brain mechanisms make the sufferer feel bad in a particular way. This special type of pain is called separation distress or panic. The biological value of this type of pain is that *it motivates the sufferer to avoid separation, and to seek reunion with the lost object*. However, if this biologically desirable outcome fails to materialise, then a second mechanism kicks in, which shuts down the distress and causes the lost individual to *give up*. This giving up is the "despair" phase of social loss (Panksepp et al., 1989, 1991).

This system is embodied in a well-defined network of brain structures (Figure 3.1), starting in the anterior cingulate gyrus (about which so much has been said in recent neuro-imaging studies and deep brain stimulation treatments of depression (Mayberg et al., 2005)), coursing downwards through various thalamic, hypothalamic, and other basal forebrain nuclei, terminating in the ancient midbrain (pain generating) neurons of the periaqueductal grey. Activation and deactivation of this system is fundamentally mediated by opioid receptors. *Mu*-opioid agonists, in particular, activate it in such a way as to generate feelings of secure wellbeing that are the very opposite of depression, whereas *mu*-opioid blockade or withdrawal produces separation distress. This state is most readily identified in animal models by distress vocalisations (Panksepp, 1998). Bowlby (1980) classically described this phenotype as "protest" behaviour, which he contrasted with the more chronic "despair" behaviours that immediately follow on from it. The transition from acute "protest" to chronic

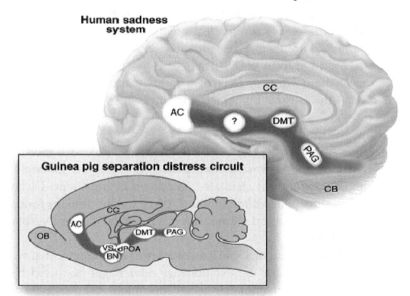

Figure 3.1. There are striking similarities between regions of the guinea pig brain that mediate separation distress and areas of the human brain that are activated by feelings of sadness (Source: Solms & Panksepp, 2010).
Note: AC = anterior cingulate; VS = ventral septum; dPOA = dorsal preoptic area; BN = bed nucleus of the stria terminalis; DMT = dorsomedial thalamus; PAG = periaqueductal central; OB = olfactory bulb; CC = corpus callosum; CB = cerebellum.

"despair" presumably evolved to protect the separated animal from metabolic exhaustion, or, alternatively, to deflect the attention of predators, or both. In other words, *it positively motivates the animal to give up.*

It is the "despair" phenotype that seems most closely to resemble clinical depression (Harris, 1989). The separation distress system, which is greatly sensitised by the floods of hormones (oestrogen, progesterone) and peptides (prolactin, oxytocin) that precede child-birth and facilitate maternal care, developed early in mammalian evolution. This is why the mechanisms which mediate attachment and separation are much more sensitive in females, who are more than twice as likely as males to suffer from depression. How do serotonin theorists account for this significant fact?

We have also known for a long time that the chemicals that mediate the brain's separation–attachment mechanism (opioids) have powerful antidepressant properties (Bodkin et al., 1996). If it were not for the addictive risks of opiates, they would almost certainly have formed the front line of antidepression medications. In fact, there is good reason to believe that the natural brain chemi-cals—endorphins—that make us feel good when we are safely and securely attached are themselves addictive; in short, that affectionate bonds are a primal form of addiction. This system apparently pro-vides the elemental means by which mother and infant attach to each other—the means by which they become addicted to one another.

Although these opioid-driven attachment systems might be the pivotal mechanism in depression, there are many associated mecha-nisms that mediate the various depressive subtypes. For example, kappa opioid (dynorphin) facilitated shutdown of dopamine-driven appetitive systems (when an individual "gives up" in despair) forms an independent aetiological mechanism in a majority of cases (Nestler & Carlezon, 2006).

It seems that the pain of social loss and defeat are the price that we mammals had to pay for the evolutionary advantages bestowed by this system, that is, by mammalian social attachment, the prototype of which is the mother–infant bond. This is an instance of a more general principle: conscious feelings, both positive and negative, evolved because they enhance survival and reproductive success. This is their causal role.

Neuropsychoanalysis

The evolutionary processes that gave rise to such emotional endophe-notypes do not coincide with their higher cortical representations, let alone with their experiential end-products.

An infant in the grip of separation distress does not consciously think, "This loss of my beloved mother is bad for me because it endangers my survival and thereby reduces my reproductive fitness". What the individual feels might *ultimately* serve the interests of the species, but the individual organism experiences only itself, not the biological mechanisms that gave rise to it. The infant simply feels bad, and then thinks something like, "This loss of my beloved mother is bad; I want her back". Or it feels, "This loss of my mother is bad; I hate it . . . so I hate her."

Individuals are motivated primarily by subjective feelings, and secondarily by subjective thoughts, not by objective mechanisms. This is true even if the objective mechanisms *explain* the subjective feelings and thoughts in question. Here is a more complex example: the objective mechanism of the "despair" phase of the separation response appears to be a shutdown of the "protest" phase, with its associated SEEKING impulses. This prevents metabolic exhaustion, the risk of attracting predatory interest, and the dangers of straying too far. At the neurochemical level, this shutdown is probably mediated by dynorphin blockade of dopamine arousal, which (in behaviourist terms) replaces positive approach behaviours with negative withdrawal behaviours. In learning-theory terms, the seeking of "rewards" elicits "punishment" responses. This also involves frustration of SEEKING desires, which normally elicits RAGE responses (Panksepp, 1998). The RAGE responses must, therefore, be inhibited, or even reversed. Subjectively, this mechanism is reflected in the fact that hope is replaced by hopelessness, leading to anhedonia, or, worse, hope is replaced by an attack on the self. The subjective outcome is, thus, quite different from the objective mechanism: "shut down SEEKING to promote survival" becomes "I hate the part of me that needs her and hopes she will come back" (cf. the so-called "negative therapeutic reaction").

The fact that such a process might, at the representational (neocortical) level, involve an attack upon an internalised frustrating object is neither here nor there. The objective mechanism that explains (and ultimately causes) this state of affairs is the survival advantage of a shift from "protest" to "despair". The subjective experience of this shift—a loss of self-esteem or, worse, self-hatred—is entirely ignorant of the underlying mechanism, *but it motivates the organism to behave in the way that it does.*

I am not suggesting drugs or deep brain stimulation are the ways we should treat depression, but the drugs that actually work *prove the concept.* This is why it is interesting to be able to report that, recently, Panksepp and colleagues (Coenen et al., 2011) have developed a successful surgical intervention for intractable major depression by inserting a deep brain stimulator directly into the SEEKING system, thereby reversing the separation distress shutdown response described above. Likewise, he and colleagues (Yovell et al., 2016) successfully treated suicidal patients with Buprenorphine, the relatively safe opiate that Bodkin used (see above), which acts directly on the PANIC system. And he had dramatic results. None of his patients killed themselves, their mood lifted, and this was sustained over the period of time that he studied them. It made sense to use Buprenorphine on these patients, not only because suicidality clearly has more to do with the "protest" phase of the separation distress cascade, but also because, ethically, in such cases, you cannot sit around for three weeks waiting for SSRIs to work—if they do work.

We neuropsychoanalysts are, therefore, formulating hypotheses which led to the development of neurosurgical and psychopharmacological treatments, arising out of an understanding that these feelings in the symptom complex called depression *mean* something; that depression arises in relation to a specific kind of social context, a biological situation of universal significance. The brain chemistries mediating these brain circuits therefore mean something, too. They respond to a particular social situation, a particular psychological constellation, a particular type of object relation (loss). That is what triggers this mechanism. The power of the neuropsychoanalytical approach is that the gap between a psychopharmacological understanding and a psychotherapeutic understanding is reduced dramatically. They do not become competing ways of understanding what is going on; they just become alternative ways of treating what is going on—complementary ways of treating what is going on. We should also recall that not all patients are amenable to psychoanalysis, especially not chronically depressed and suicidal patients.

Conclusion

So why does depression feel bad? It feels bad, according to affective neuroscience and neuropsychoanalysis, for two reasons: first, to encourage us to form attachments, particularly to early caring figures, but also with our sexual mates and offspring and social groups and the like; second, to persuade us to give up hope if our attempts to reunite with such figures or groups do not succeed within a limited time-frame, when we have become detached (or lost). The aetiological fact that such feelings can be too easily provoked, or too difficult to erase, etc., in some individuals, is immaterial to the biological forces that selected them into the mammalian genome in the first place.

In the light of the existence of brain structures that generate such feelings, it seems reasonable to at least hypothesise that the linchpin of depression is none of the things that have so preoccupied contemporary psychiatric researchers over the past three decades, but, rather, the evolutionarily conserved brain state that mediates the transition from "protest" to "despair" in the wake of social loss. In other words, it seems reasonable to hypothesise that the core brain basis of depression revolves around the process by which separation distress is normally shut down (possibly by kappa-opioids like dynorphin), prompting the animal to "give up".

Why are mainstream psychiatric researchers not investigating the role of these candidate brain processes in depression? They seem to be the obvious place to start, if we are going to take the phenomenology of depression itself (as opposed to things that correlate with it) as our starting point, as we in neuropsychoanalysis have.

We believe that such obvious starting points are neglected due to an ongoing, deep prejudice against acknowledging the implications for science of the subjective nature of feelings, and their causal efficacy in the brain. This prejudice is most unfortunate, because subjective feelings certainly exist, and they almost certainly evolved for a reason (they almost certainly enhanced reproductive fitness).

Feelings are, accordingly, almost certainly a central feature of how the brain works. Therefore, we ignore them at our peril.

Notes

1. It is important to note, though, that even this step is disallowed by many scientists when it comes to non-human animals. It is still widely considered anthropomorphist to infer conscious states from the behaviour of animals who cannot verbally "declare" their feelings. How can they seriously believe that feelings are uniquely human, that affect emerged in evolution only with the appearance of human beings!
2. Freud used the term "Trauer" which Strachey translated as "mourning", but which can also be translated as "grief".

References

Berger, M., Gray, J. A., & Roth, B. L. (2009). The expanded biology of serotonin. *Annual Review of Medicine, 60*: 355–366.

Bodkin, J. A., Zornberg, G. L., Lukas, S. E., & Cole, J. O. (1995). Buprenorphine treatment of refractory depression. *Journal of Clinical Psychopharmacology, 15*: 49–57.

Bowlby, J. (1980). *Loss: Sadness and Depression.* New York: Basic Books.

Coenen, V. A., Schlaepfer, T. E., Maedler, B., & Panksepp, J. (2011). Cross-species affective functions of the medial forebrain bundle-implications for the treatment of affective pain and depression in humans. *Neuroscience & Biobehavioral Reviews, 35*: 1971–1981.

De Kloet, E., Joels, M., & Holsboer, F. (2005). Stress and the brain: from adaptation to disease. *Nature Reviews Neuroscience, 6*: 463–475.

Delgado, P. L., Charney, D. S., Price, L. H., Aghajanian, G. K., Landis, H., & Heninger, G. R. (1990). Serotonin function and the mechanism of antidepressant action: reversal of antidepressant-induced remission by rapid depletion of plasma tryptophan. *Archives of General Psychiatry, 47*: 411–418.

Freud, S. (1917e). Mourning and melancholia. *S. E., 14*: 239–258. London: Hogarth.

Freud, S. (1940a). *An Outline of Psychoanalysis. S. E., 23*: 144–207. London: Hogarth.

Harris, J. C. (1989). Experimental animal modeling of depression and anxiety. *Psychiatric Clinics of North America, 18*: 815–836.

Harro, J., & Oreland, L. (2001). Depression as a spreading adjustment disorder of monoaminergic neurons: a case for primary implications of the locus coeruleus. *Brain Research Reviews, 38*: 79–128.

Heim, C., & Nemeroff, C. (1999). The impact of early adverse experiences on brain systems involved in the pathophysiology of anxiety and affective disorders. *Biological Psychiatry, 46*: 1509–1522.

Koziek, M., Middlemas, D., & Bylund, D. (2008). Brain-derived neurotrophic factor and its receptor tropomyosin-related kinase B in the mechanism of action of antidepressant therapies. *Phamacology & Therapeutics, 117*: 30–51.

Levinson, D. F. (2006). The genetics of depression: a review. *Biological Psychiatry, 60*: 84–92.

Mayberg, H., Lozano, A., Voon, V., McNeely, H., Seminowicz, D., Hamani, C., Schwalb, J., & Kennedy, S. (2005). Deep brain stimulation for treatment-resistant depression. *Neuron, 45*: 651–660.

McEwen, B. S. (2000). The neurobiology of stress: from serendipity to clinical relevance. *Brain Research, 886*(1–2): 172–189.

McEwen, B. S. (2007). Physiology and neurobiology of stress and adaptation: central role of the brain. *Physiological Reviews, 87*: 873–904.

Nestler, E. J., & Carlezon, W. A. Jr. (2006). The mesolimbic dopamine reward circuit in depression. *Biological Psychiatry, 59*: 1151–1159.

Panksepp, J. (1998). *Affective Neuroscience: The Foundations of Human and Animal Emotion.* New York: Oxford University Press.

Panksepp, J. (2003a). Can anthropomorphic analyses of "separation cries" in other animals inform us about the emotional nature of social loss in humans? *Psychological Reviews, 110*: 376–388.

Panksepp, J. (2003b). Feeling the pain of social loss. *Science, 302*: 237–239.

Panksepp, J. (2005). Feelings of social loss: the evolution of pain and the ache of a broken heart. In: R. Ellis & N. Newton (Eds.), *Consciousness & Emotions* (pp. 23–55). Amsterdam: John Benjamins.

Panksepp, J., Lensing, P., & Bernatzky, G. (1989). Delta and kappa opiate receptor control of separation distress. *Neuroscience Abstracts, 15*: 845.

Panksepp, J., Yates, G., Ikemoto, S., & Nelson, E. (1991). Simple ethological models of depression: social-isolation induced "despair" in chicks and mice. In: B. Olivier & J. Moss (Eds.), *Animal Models in Psychopharmacology* (pp. 161–181). Holland: Duphar.

Pryce, C. R., Ruedi-Bettschen, D., Dettling, A. C., Weston, A., Russig, H., Ferger, B., & Feldon, J. (2005). Long-term effects of early-life environmental manipulations in rodents and primates: potential animal models in depression research. *Neuroscience and Biobehavioral Reviews, 29*: 649–674.

Sacks, O. (1984) *A Leg to Stand On.* New York: Pantheon.

Schildkraut, J. (1965). The catecholamine hypothesis of affective disorders: a review of supportive evidence. *American Journal of Psychiatry, 122*: 509–522.

Solms, M. (in press). The scientific standing of psychoanalysis. *British Journal of Psychiatry International*.

Solms, M., & Panksepp, J. (2010). Why depression feels bad. In: E. Perry, D. Collerton, F. LeBeau, & H. Ashton (Eds.), *New Horizons in the Neuroscience of Consciousness* (pp. 169–179). Amsterdam: John Benjamins.

Watt, D., & Panksepp, J. (2009). Depression: an evolutionarily conserved mechanism to terminate separation distress? A review of aminergic, peptidergic, and neural network perspectives. *Neuropsychoanalysis, 11*(1): 7–51.

Yovell, Y., Bar, G., Mashiah, M., Baruch, Y., Briskman, I., Asherov, J., Lotan, A., Rigbi, A., & Panksepp, J. (2016). Ultra-low-dose buprenorphine as a time-limited treatment for severe suicidal ideation: a randomized controlled trial. *American Journal of Psychiatry, 173*: 491–498.

Zellner, M., Watt, D., Solms, M., & Panksepp, J. (2011). Affective neuroscientific and neuropsychoanalytic approaches to two intractable psychiatric problems: why depression feels so bad and what addicts really want. *Neuroscience & Biobehavioral Reviews, 35*: 2000–2008.

Zupancic, M., & Guilleminault, C. (2006). Agomelatine: a preliminary review of a new antidepressant. *CNS Drugs, 20*: 981–992.

CHAPTER FOUR

The case study in neuropsychoanalysis: a bridge between the objective and the subjective?*

Christian E. Salas, Martin Casassus, and Oliver H. Turnbull

What is neuropsychoanalysis?

Neuropsychoanalysis has been described as an interdisciplinary field that attempts to generate links between psychoanalytic schools and the neurosciences, or as an attempt to insert psychoanalysis into the neurosciences (Solms & Turnbull, 2011). If we consider the place of neuropsychoanalysis in the history of the neurosciences, it could be argued that its emergence is a response to the surprising omission, by cognitive neuropsychology and cognitive neuroscience in general, of emotion as a core aspect of mental life (Turnbull, 2001).

Let us consider a few examples to illustrate this point. In the *Encyclopedia of the Human Brain* (Ramachandran, 2002), from its 330 topics only seven (anger, aggression, anxiety, depression, emotion, laughter and humour, and mood disorders) are directly related to the central issue of emotion, a mere two per cent of the manuscript. Higher mental functions, such as perception and cognition, in contrast, occupy

* Previously published as "A neuropsychoanalytic approach to case studies" in *Clinical Social Work Journal*, 3 August 2016. Thanks to Springer for the permission to reprint.

thirty-eight per cent of the text, with 125 entries (see Figure 4.1). A similar picture can be observed in the handbook *Fundamentals of Human Neuropsychology* (Kolb & Whishaw, 2009), where only one chapter is devoted to emotion, hardly occupying four per cent of the book. This position might reflect the status of emotion within cognitive neuroscience, but it entirely fails to capture the importance of emotion when viewed from other perspectives. Notably, classic and new *affective* approaches to the neuroscience of mental life (Cory & Gardner, 2002; Damasio, 2012; Panksepp, 1998) have offered important evidence to position emotion not only as *primary* (i.e., it develops first in phylogenetic and ontogenetic terms) but also as *hierarchically* pre-eminent (i.e., earlier developed systems are more emotionally powerful, and their damage compromises all other systems above them in the hierarchy).

Neuropsychoanalysis has been a key actor in bringing emotion into the mind–brain debate, and its main contributions can be described as both theoretical and technical. In theoretical terms, it has introduced key ideas from psychoanalysis to neuroscience regarding the emotional and instinctual basis of the human mind, thus challenging "cognitive" or "top-down" views of the mind–brain problem (Cromwell & Panksepp, 2011). The description of basic motivational,

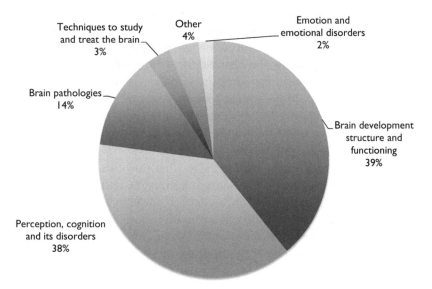

Figure 4.1. The predominance of a cognitive view of the mind in the neurosciences (Source: Ramachandran, 2002).

or instinctual, systems, which influence higher order cognitive processes, such as learning and thinking, is, here, the most impressive example (Panksepp, 1998; Panksepp & Solms, 2012). In technical terms, neuropsychoanalysis has provided important tools to explore the subjective side of the mind–brain problem (what it feels like to be a mind), something that has been elusive in the traditional third person methodologies employed by neuroscience. The use of the psychoanalytic method to observe changes in emotion, motivation, and personality after focal brain injury (Kaplan-Solms & Solms, 2000), what initially was known as depth neuropsychology (Turnbull & Solms, 2004), is perhaps the best example of this type of influence.

There are other fields that have evolved from, or been influenced by, the psychoanalytic study of brain injured patients.[1] However, they do not use case studies as their main methodological approach. Psychodynamic neuroscience, for example, is a specialised field that focuses on generating and testing predictions of classic metapsychological models by using the multi-method approach of modern neuroscience (Fotopoulou et al., 2012). Even though psychodynamic neuroscience observations are inspired by psychoanalytic theory, and use brain injured patients as main object of study, they are mainly derived from the use of rigorously controlled experimental paradigms and do not occur in the context of the analytic setting, as depth neuropsychological case studies do. The field of affective neuroscience has also been influenced by ideas derived from neuropsychoanalysis. This is not a surprise, considering that affective neuroscience focuses on the "neurological understanding of the basic emotional operating systems of the mammalian brain and the various *conscious* and *unconscious* internal states they generate" (Panksepp, 1998, p. 5). Most of the early findings generated by this field have been based on animal studies. However, during the past decade, and due to a fruitful partnership between Jaak Panksepp and Mark Solms, psychoanalytic ideas derived from lesion studies have been integrated with animal data in order to draft a more comprehensive model of the mental apparatus (Panksepp & Solms, 2012; Solms & Panksepp, 2012).

The case study in neuropsychoanalysis: historical influences

As the reader might expect, the historical development of both the neurosciences and the psychoanalyses have shaped the way in which neuropsychoanalysis has understood case studies. Nevertheless, there is one common factor that lies at the dawn of both disciplines, which has determined the way in which case studies are conceived: the clinico–anatomical method. In this section, we describe how this method shaped the work of twentieth century neuroscientists and briefly comment on how it also influenced Freud's approach to the mind–brain problem (for a more detailed historic account on the relevance of this method for both neuroscience and psychoanalysis, see Kaplan-Solms & Solms, 2000).

The clinico–anatomical method has been described as the circular process that allows brain function to be inferred by studying the correspondence between clinical manifestations and lesion location (Catani et al., 2012). Tracing the historical origins of this method, Solms comments that

> This method was used by internal medicine in order to diagnose and treat diseases attacking the interior of the body, which could not be directly apprehended in the patient, but had to be inferred from their indirect manifestations as external symptoms and signs. With the accumulation of experience, over generations, it gradually became possible for the internal physician to recognize pathognomonic constellations of symptoms and signs and thereby to predict from the clinical presentation what and where the underlying disease process was, and to conduct the treatment accordingly. (2000a, pp. 76–77)

It was thanks to neurologists in the middle of the nineteenth century, who were trained in the clinico–anatomical method employed by internal medicine, that such technical approaches began to be used in exploring pathologies of the brain and developing theories regarding the localisation of mental functions (Riese, 1959). With the progressive development of neurology as a separate field, case studies using the clinico–anatomical method became a major source of insights regarding the neural basis of a wide range of psychological processes. By using this approach, it was possible for clinicians to determine how damage to discrete areas of the brain was correlated to clinical syndromes, or specific constellations of changes in mental processes. Thus, the seminal works on expressive and receptive aphasia by Broca and Wernicke paved the way for many other case studies that described the clinico–anatomical correlations of a wide variety of functions, such as acalculia (Gerstmann, 1940), apraxia (Liepmann,

1908), neglect (Brain, 1941) or anosognosia (Babinski, 1914). As noted by Solms (2000b, pp. 78–79), "by 1934, this approach had produced a detailed map of the psychological functions of the various cortical convolutions, including such complex faculties as the body schema, emotional sensations and the social ego". These findings marked the beginning of a new sub discipline, commonly known as behavioural neurology, which later developed into the modern discipline of neuropsychology (Kaplan-Solms & Solms, 2000).

Even though this method provided a useful tool to systematically explore, for the first time, the mind–brain problem, its limitations were pointed out by a (psychoanalytically minded) Soviet psychologist, Alexandr Luria. Luria's work can be considered a response to the "narrow" localisationism that emerged from initial clinico–anatomical studies, which attempted to "localize complex mental function directly in local areas of the brain" (Luria, 1976, pp. 22–23). He showed that elementary physiological functions, such as cutaneous sensation, vision, hearing, or movement were clearly represented in defined areas of the cortex. However, more complex forms of mental activity, such as language or problem solving, were organised in a far more distributed manner. Luria proposed that these complex forms of mental activity should be, rather, conceptualised as organised systems of concertedly working zones, each of which performs its role in complex functional systems, and which may be located in completely different and often far distant areas of the brain (1976, p. 31). The idea of a brain composed of functional systems, which depend on interacting components that are widely distributed in the brain, and where each of them contributes with a very specific ability, is a key aspect of what gives Luria's theory the name of dynamic neuropsychology. This movement from a "narrow" to a more "dynamic" localisationism generated important changes in how case studies were conceived, for a number of reasons (Luria, 1968, 1972).

First, the complexity of systems meant that case studies became in-depth explorations, since not only the most obvious deficits caused by the injury had to be considered. Most importantly, all the other associated symptoms had to be carefully pondered. In other words, a picture of the complete syndrome that emerged with the injury had to be generated, in order to determine the common factor that was compromised by damage to a specific brain area and expressed itself in different domains of performance. As noted by Luria himself:

[This] is an accepted method in clinical medicine, where the thought-ful physician is never interested merely in the course of a disease he happens to be studying at the moment, but tries to determine what effect a disturbance of one particular process has on the other organic processes; how changes in the latter (which ultimately have one root cause) alter the activity of the entire organism, thus giving rise to the total *picture of disease*, to what medicine commonly terms as *syndrome*. The study of syndromes, however, need not be restricted to clinical medicine. By the same token one can analyse how an unusually devel-oped feature of psychic make up produces changes, which are causally related to it, in the entire structure of psychic life, in the total personality. In the latter instance, too, we would be dealing with "syndromes", having one causal factor, except that they would be psychological rather than clinical syndromes. (Luria, 1968)

A second important implication of adopting this dynamic approach was that case studies had to explore both the way in which individuals *successfully* performed a specific task and how they *failed* to perform it. In other words, the idea of behaviour as a "process" became more relevant than behaviour as "output"—whether the indi-vidual accomplishes a certain task or not.[2] As a consequence, clini-cians became interested in the analysis of errors, and the process by which a patient reaches a solution to a problem. Even though many neuropsychologists link "process" analysis to Boston based neuropsy-chologists of the 1960s and 1970s, such as Edith Kaplan and Norman Geschwind (Libon et al., 2013), or with the work of Luria (Luria & Majovski, 1977), it is arguably Kurt Goldstein who first brought atten-tion to this relevant issue (Goldstein, 1925/1971; Luria, 1966a). In his seminal book, *The Organism*, Goldstein comments on the logic of case studies and syndrome analysis:

In depth case studies allow a thorough analysis of the causes of effects, of success and failure on a given task . . . If we regard a reaction only from the standpoint of the actual solution of a task, we may overlook the deviation from normality, because the individual completes the task by a detour that may not be evident in the solution. Only accu-rate analysis, through an examination that makes it impossible for the patient to achieve a result in a roundabout way, can disclose the defect . . . Equally ambiguous are the negative results of a medical examina-tion. The wrong response is too often judged to be a simple failure, whereas actually, under careful analysis, it may throw considerable light on the mental functions of the patient. Only by this means can we discover whether there really is a defect in the ability demanded by the task or whether the patient has failed only because of special circumstances induced by the task situation. (Goldstein, 1995, p. 40)

Unfortunately, Luria did not manage to use his dynamic approach to explore the neural basis of non-cognitive, or emotional, mental processes. In fact, in *Higher Cortical Mental Functions in Man* (1966b), his most important work, he referred only to emotional changes in relation to damage to thalamic or hypothalamic regions, or briefly described them when discussing the akinetic–abulic syndrome, which is commonly observed after damage to the anterior divisions of the brain. Nevertheless, Luria was quite aware of the relevance of such processes, as is clear in the closing chapter of *The Working Brain*:

Neuropsychology is still a very young science, taking its very first step, and a period of thirty years is not a very long time for the development of any science. That is why some very important chapters, such as *motives, complex forms of emotions* and the *structure of personality* are not included in this book. Perhaps they will be added in future editions. (1976, pp. 341–342)

It is interesting to turn our attention at this point to psychoanalysis, since the work of Freud also evolved to a dynamic view of the mind, very similar to that put forward by Luria. Nevertheless, Freud did not manage to benefit from Luria's dynamic localisationism, thus remaining only on a purely psychological level of analysis to understand emotional and motivational processes. As the reader might well know, Freud was initially a neurologist, well trained in the clinico–anatomical method. However, as he attempted to use such a method to understand the neuroses,[3] he became aware of its limitations. As a consequence, he began to conceptualise these pathologies as disorders of psychological *function* as opposed to anatomical *structure* (Solms & Saling, 1986). As noted by Solms (2000b):

In addition to conceptualizing mental process as dynamic, functional terms (as opposed to static, anatomical ones) he would conceive of mental functions in purely psychological terms (as opposed to physiological ones); and accordingly, he would recognize them as being unlocalizable in the tissues of the brain. Henceforth, for the reminder of his scientific life, Freud would speak of mental processes not as being localized in the elements of the mental organ, but rather as being distributed; that is as being located not within, but rather between the elements. (p. 86)

It was this shift to a psychological and dynamic model of the mind that allowed Freud to explore complex forms of mental activity such as the unconscious, defence mechanisms, and the structure of the personality (ego, id, superego). Exactly the same aspects of the human mind that Luria recognised as missing in his theory and which he, later in life, described as a necessary object of future investigation. However, as noted above, Freud was not aware of Luria's modifications to the clinico–anatomical method (his "dynamic" neuropsychology), modifications that would have made possible the exploration of complex forms of mental activity, even those that occur deep in the mental apparatus (Solms, 2000b). It can be said that the need to draw together these two traditions is the seed that brings neuropsychoanalysis into existence. Thus, neuropsychoanalysis is born as an attempt to apply Luria's dynamic neuropsychology in the study of emotion, motivation, and personality. It is this same convergence that accounts for the initial name coined for neuropsychoanalysis: depth neuropsychology.

As the reader can realise from this historical review, Freudian ideas have been a predominant influence in the development of neuropsychoanalysis. This responds to both theoretical and technical reasons. Theoretically speaking, Freud's metapsychology, and his tripartite model, ego, superego, and id, offered an extremely useful conceptual framework to explore changes in emotion, motivation, and personality after brain injury. In technical terms, Freud's uni-personal model of the mind presented a natural fit with neuroscientific theories and methods, which considered the isolated individual—his brain and internal "mechanisms"—as main units of analysis (Salas, 2014). However, other psychoanalytic strands have also influenced neuropsychoanalysis. In clinical studies itself, for example, Kaplan-Solms and Solms used object relational (Kleinian) ideas to explore personality changes after damage to the right hemisphere. More recently, several authors have turned to contemporaneous relational ideas in order to understand how brain injuries force survivors to move from intrinsic to extrinsic forms of emotion regulation (Freed, 2002; Salas, 2012; Yeates, 2009). In contrast to Freudian uni-personal psychology, relational authors propose that subjective experience is actively shaped in the context of an "interactional field" where individuals are immersed (Mitchell, 1988). Such perspective resonates strongly with relational views in neuropsychology itself, which emphasise that mental processes—cognitive and affective—emerge from, and are modulated by, the "intermental space" (Bowen et al., 2010; Leont'ev, 1981; Luria, 1963). The case study presented in this chapter draws ideas from both Freudian and relational traditions, thus following the work of several authors that have argued for a potential "common ground" between these schools (for reviews, see Wachtel, 2008; Wallerstein, 2002).

Case studies in the present

As noted above, case studies have been at the heart of the development of theory on the mind–brain relationship during the past century (Code, 1996), and have also played a central role in the generation of psychodynamic models of the mind (Kächele et al., 2012). However, the emergence of new technologies to explore the brain, as well as the dominance of quantitative methodologies to investigate the effectiveness of therapeutic interventions, have led some to question their relevance (Vandenbroucke, 1999).

In neuropsychology, both clinicians and researchers have acknowledged the advantage of using case studies. First, case studies avoid the averaging effects of group studies, where the dramatic impairments of extraordinary individuals are "washed out" by inclusion in a group (Shallice, 1988). Paradigmatic case studies like HM or DF show extreme and relatively circumscribed deficits (anterograde amnesia and object agnosia, respectively), in the presence of largely preserved general mental function (Goodale & Milner, 1992; Milner et al., 1968). Second, case studies avoid the superficial effects of group studies. All too often, group analysis consists of a modest number of tests, carried out on an impressive number of participants. Single case studies, by contrast, tend to focus on a substantial, detailed, and often custom-designed set of tests, carried out over a period of months or years on one individual. Thus, case studies gain through *depth* what they lack in *breadth*. Third, the case study is able to accommodate the vagaries of individual differences and variations of premorbid abilities. Rather than averaging a group of males and females with a mean age of fifty-five on a face recognition task, a case study can focus on the sheep face recognition ability of an unusual individual—a farmer who can no longer recognise people's faces but whose particular lifestyle has provided him with specialised skills (McNeil & Warrington, 1993). Fourth, as a method, case studies are intimately related to everyday clinical work with brain-injured patients. This is not the case for group studies, or for any other methodology. In consequence, case studies offer a more clinical-friendly method to engage practitioners in the detection and examination of potentially relevant "experiments of nature", which may contribute to the theoretical development of the mind–brain relationship (Shallice, 1979, 1988).

The development of neuroimaging technologies has raised the question of whether, with the refinement of such advanced methods, case studies will be necessary at all.[4] It has been argued by several authors that case studies cannot be replaced by data coming from neuroimaging studies, since the former offer a unique opportunity to understand the "causal role" that different brain areas have on mental functioning:

> An important goal in cognitive neuroscience is to identify the causal chain of neural events, or the mechanisms underlying cognition. The data of functional neuroimaging are correlational: a certain area is activated when certain cognitive process is occurring. Neuroimaging can never disentangle correlation from causation; in other words, it can never tell us which brain areas are casually involved in enabling a cognitive process . . . For this we must turn to studying the effects of brain damage, the 'experiments of nature' that provide a direct test of the causal role of different brain areas by showing us how the system works in their absence. Given the complementary strengths of neuroimaging and patient studies, we predict that the most successful cognitive neuroscience research programs of the twentieth-first century will be those that combine both approaches. (Feinberg & Farah, 2000, p. 17)

It is also important to mention that case studies have had a pivotal role in the treatment of the cognitive, psychological, and emotional consequences of brain damage, or what is commonly known as neuropsychological rehabilitation. As has been noted elsewhere, a "subjective turn" has occurred in neuropsychological rehabilitation, with clinicians and researchers becoming increasingly interested in quality of life and emotional adjustment as outcomes of rehabilitation efforts (Ben-Yishai & Diller, 2011; Wilson & Gracey, 2010). In this context, case studies are particularly useful to portray both the subjective experience of individuals with brain damage attempting to adjust to their cognitive and behavioural problems and the idiosyncratic nature of the rehabilitation process required by each individual (Wilson, 1999; Wilson et al., 2014). It is important to note, as a closing comment, that during the past decade, case studies have become extremely popular among clinicians and researchers as a tool to explore the efficacy of therapeutic interventions in neuropsychological rehabilitation. This methodological approach has been commonly referred to as "experimental" case study (Evans et al., 2014; McDonald, 2014; Tate et al., 2014)

We would like to close this section by addressing some methodological limitations commonly attributed to case studies (for a review on the topic, see Flyvbjerg, 2006). The first one is that the type of knowledge generated by case studies, which is concrete and practical (context-dependent) is *less valuable* than general theoretical knowledge (context-independent). If we consider the dominant scientific paradigms, the reader can easily recognise the assumption that universal laws are true knowledge in science. Even though this logic might apply to fields such as physics or chemistry, it cannot be easily extrapolated to human behaviour. Human beings become experts in a task, or activity, not by acquiring and manipulating context-independent knowledge, or a set of abstract rules, but by progressively amassing a body of knowledge based on concrete interactions with the environment. In other words, we learn, and develop theories about the world, based on situations and cases. Clinical neuropsychology is a clear example of a field where context-dependent knowledge is of paramount importance. In order to obtain their professional certification, to be considered proficient by peers in the field, clinical neuropsychologists need to demonstrate not only theoretical knowledge of the brain–mind relationship, but, more importantly, provide evidence that they can apply such knowledge in many contexts through extensive portfolios of cases. Even though context-independent and context-dependent knowledge are both necessary in this discipline, a clinical neuropsychologist is aware of the dangers of generalisation, for each case is different and no two brains are alike.

A second limitation of case studies, often suggested by those that intend to pursue the ideal of natural science in social sciences, is that they *do not offer generalisation* (Nissen & Wynn, 2014). In other words, no context-independent knowledge can be derived from them (Flyvbjerg, 2006). In order to answer to this limitation, it is important first to point to recent evidence suggesting that even experimental and correlational studies in psychological science are far from offering this sought-after generalisability. For example, in a recent study from the Open Science Collaboration (2015), 100 experiments were replicated. Remarkably, a large portion of replications produced weaker evidence for the original findings, despite using the same materials, methodology, and high statistical power. Evidence from this study suggests that the problem of generalisability might not be restricted to case studies, but, rather, reflects the inherent difficulties of studying human behaviour. In this context, however, neuropsychology has been a clear example where case studies have contributed to the development of theory and new avenues of research. As noted by many authors, for true intellectual advancement (proposing new problems, new solutions, or new ideas), case studies greatly surpass "confirmatory" methodologies (Nissen & Wynn, 2014; Vandenbroucke, 1999).

Furthermore, case studies of individuals with brain damage have been extremely relevant also in the scientific process of "falsification", by finding "black swans" that force a review of assumptions that have previously been considered as true by the scientific community. It has also been suggested by authors that the use of a series of case studies, or case-series designs, can overcome some of the limitation of single-case studies, thus contributing further to theory testing and controlling for inter-patient variations (Lambon Ralph et al., 2011).

The case study in neuropsychoanalysis: a bridge between subjective and objective aspects of the mind–brain

In the previous section, we have advanced the idea that a neuropsychoanalytic approach to case studies implies the examination of emotional, motivational, and personality changes in individuals with focal brain damage, especially by using a "dynamic" localisationist method in the context of a psychoanalytic treatment. By taking brain-injured patients into psychoanalysis, or psychodynamic psychotherapy,[5] it is possible to determine how different functions of the mental apparatus (e.g., ego, id, superego) have been affected by a specific lesion. These observed changes then can be correlated with the brain area damaged, as well as with other "objective" sources of evidence, such as neuropsychological assessments. Such correlation reveals the contribution of the part of the brain that is damaged to the organisation of that mental function. As a next step, these hypotheses are checked against the observation of other patients with similar lesions, thus determining patterns of association between brain regions and mental functions of psychoanalytic interest. According to Turnbull and Solms (2004), this method allows a bridge between the subjective and objective views of the mind–brain, or first and third person observations:

> The advantage of such an approach is that it allows one and the same thing to be simultaneously studied from both the psychoanalytic and the neuroscientific perspectives, so that the two sets of observations, and the resultant theoretical accounts, refer to the same reality. Only this enables us to link the subjective and objective approaches in mind/brain realities rather than merely semantic constructs. (Turnbull & Solms, 2004, pp. 573–574)

The potential relevance of a neuropsychoanalytic approach to the relationship between subjective and objective aspects of the mind–brain could be substantial, since the link between both psychical and physical gulfs (as poetically explained by Sacks) has been for decades a challenging task for researchers (Northoff & Heinzel, 2006; Northoff et al., 2007; Varela & Shear, 1999a). In other words, how can the person's subjective state (first-person subjective data) be linked with the person's neuronal state (third-person objective data)? This linkage is exactly what a neuropsychoanalytic approach to case studies potentially offers, by allowing the simultaneous observation of the same "thing" from both a psychoanalytic and a neuroscientific perspective. By psychoanalytically exploring the inner lives of individuals that have acquired brain damage, we can access their self-report of subjective states, which provides unique evidence of how the brain injury has changed the organisation of their minds (Panksepp & Solms, 2012). More importantly, by using a psychodynamic framework, which considers the observation of relational patters between therapist and client [transference and countertransference], we are also able to determine how the brain injury has changed not only inner experience, but also the patient's capacity to relate to other minds (Freed, 2002; Yeates, 2013).

According to Varela and Shear (1999a,b), a link between first- and third-person perspectives is only possible via the use of an intermediate mediation, or a second-person position. By mediation, the authors refer to

> another person that provides a curious intermediate position between first and second position . . . a mediation is eccentric[6] to the lived experience but nevertheless takes a position of one who has been there to some degree; and thus provides hints and further training. (1999b, p. 8)

Even though Varela and Shear offer this description with meditation in mind as a model technique, their observations can also apply to the role of the therapist in a psychoanalytic setting of relational nature. The therapist cannot directly access the subjective experience of the patient, but he is curious to explore it. He is also empathic to the patient's position, since he has been there himself, observing his own lived experience. In consequence, he can offer advice as to how internal life can be explored, and how contents that emerge from such exploration can be dealt with. If we consider recent developments in psychoanalytic technique (Beebe & Lachman, 2003), Varela and Shear's description of the second-person position is similar to relational views on the therapist–patient interaction. According to relational views, the therapist is not a neutral observer, but an active agent who contributes to the shaping of the patient's moment-by-moment subjective experience:

> Here in the second-person position, one gives up explicitly his/her detachments to become identified with the kind of understanding and internal coherence of his source. In fact, that is how he sees his role: as an empathic resonator with experiences that are familiar to him and which find in himself a resonant chord . . . Examples of this position abound in the traditions that we have examined in the sphere of human practices. The position here is not that of a neutral anthropologist; it is rather one of a coach or a midwife. His/her trade is grounded in the sensitivity to the subtle indices of his interlocutor's phrasing, bodily language and expressiveness, seeking for indices (more or less explicit), which are inroads into the *common* experiential ground. (Varela & Shear, 1999b, p. 10)

The question of how this "second-person position" should be implemented when working with brain injured patients is a technical problem of extreme relevance, but points in directions far beyond the scope of this chapter. Nevertheless, a couple of ideas seem especially relevant. The first relates to the fact that the therapist can be biased in many ways when facilitating the exploration of the patient's subjective or lived experience. This is inevitable, since therapist and patient co-construct the intersubjective space where they relate. In consequence, the therapist's biases can be observed during moments when he interrupts chains of associations, saturates patients' descriptions, assumes that he knows what the patient means or feels without checking, over interprets contents offered by the patient, unconsciously resists the exploration of certain areas of the patient's inner experience, or simply distorts the perception of the patient's feelings, behaviours, or cognitions. Here, we believe that supervision, as a space that allows the observation and revision of the process by which the therapist facilitates patients' exploration of their inner experience, is key. In fact, supervision can also be considered to belong to a second-person perspective, but one where the experience of the therapist becomes the focus. A supervisor is eccentric to the lived experience of the therapist, but is in a position of one who has been there before and who is able to offer advice.

A second technical matter of great importance when working with brain-injured patients is how introspection can be supported in consideration of the patient's cognitive impairments. How can we help individuals with difficulties in finding words, or who are concrete or tangential in their way of thinking, to focus on their inner experience and perhaps offer richer descriptions? How much support is necessary in order to facilitate introspection, and how can we be sure we are not saturating the patient's descriptions with our personal views? Here, we believe that insights from studies interviewing individuals with communicative and cognitive problems after brain damage are extremely useful in offering insights to adjust therapeutic tools in order to facilitate introspection (Carlsson et al., 2007; Paterson & Scott-Findlay, 2002).

A brief neuropsychoanalytic case study on changes in ego function after left dorso-medial prefrontal damage

We would like to illustrate the logic of the neuropsychoanalytic approach by briefly describing the case of Professor F (Salas et al.,

2014). Professor F was a seventy-two-year-old man, married, and a father of three. In 2006, he suffered an ischemic stroke of the left anterior and middle cerebral arteries, damaging the medial part of the left dorsal prefrontal cortex and the intraparietal cortex (see Figure 4.2). Before the accident, Professor F worked in academia as a social science lecturer. After the stroke, he presented with an expressive aphasia and right hemiparesis, which evolved positively during the first months. Later on, during outpatient rehabilitation, a moderate dysexecutive disorder was diagnosed. Professor F spontaneously complained about difficulties managing time fatigue and high levels of anxiety. He also mentioned being forgetful, unable to focus, and with moments where his mind was blank. Formal assessment suggested a mild aphasia, as well as deficits in information processing, working memory, cognitive flexibility, planning, and monitoring. This profile of dysexecutive impairment had persisted for almost ten years, and was characterised by a marked deficit in cognitive flexibility, and a mild difficulty in initiation.

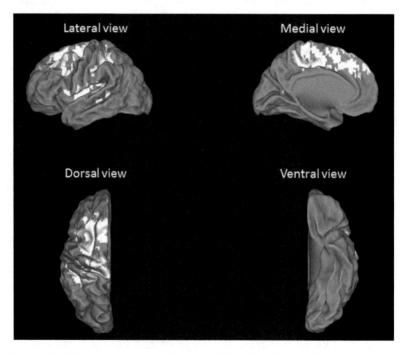

Figure 4.2.   3D reconstruction of Professor F's lesion (Source: Salas et al., 2014).

Since the beginning of outpatient rehabilitation, Professor F has been treated by one of the authors (CS), who is a clinical neuropsychologist and psychoanalytic psychotherapist. The treatment has extended for over eight years, and a rich corpus of material in the form of therapist's notes and recordings has been accumulated. We would like to use this material in order to portray the subjective experience of Professor F after the injury (first-person perspective) and correlate it with evidence from his neuropsychological assessment and neuroimaging data (third-person perspective). The main neuropsychoanalytic hypothesis that we would like to put forward, is that damage to the left dorso-medial PFC, and its associated cognitive impairments, alters the Ego's ability to use preconscious verbal thinking in the regulation of feelings.

Traditionally, the left dorso-medial PFC has been functionally associated to *cognitive* processes, and authors have proposed that any change in emotion that might occur after damage to this brain region is *secondary* to the cognitive deficits that emerge from it (Anderson & Tranel, 2002). From a syndrome approach, damage to the dorsolateral surface often generates a wide array of symptoms, such as deficits in verbal working memory and set shifting (changing from one mental representation to another) while energisation problems (initiating and sustaining responses when there is no external stimuli reminding the patient to stay engaged in the task) are common after damage to the more dorso-medial portion of the left PFC (Stuss & Alexander, 2007). In sum, it is possible to say that this area contributes at least two "cognitive" components that are key to the mental apparatus, mental flexibility and stimulus-independent thinking.

Importantly, damage to these components compromises a complex mental process that is central to psychoanalysis and extremely relevant for emotional life: preconscious verbal thinking.[7] Preconscious verbal thinking has been described as the principal tool by which the "dynamic" function of the ego, or its role as the inhibitory pole of the mind, is enacted (Kaplan-Solms & Solms, 2000). From a psychoanalytic point of view, human beings learn—through interacting with significant others—to use verbal mental representations, and attach them to somatic experiences, in order to regulate or manage feelings, or, in Freud's language, to "tame" them. Furthermore, the use of verbal representations, by which unconscious or somatic states are linked with words—symbolisation—is at the heart of the therapeutic process as understood by psychoanalysis (Freedman et al., 2011).

One of the first important neuropsychoanalytic observations in the case of Professor F is that, in moments of negative arousal, he becomes stuck in negative cognitions, and is unable to either shift away from them or decrease their intensity via the generation of positive and soothing verbal representations. As the reader can see, both problems can be considered a consequence of classic cognitive deficits in mental flexibility and stimulus-independent thinking. In these situations, Professor F appears "captured" by affects, since he is not able to manipulate his thoughts with a regulatory purpose:

> It is like a peculiar experience, like having something separated inside, what you think with your head and what you feel, and that you are not able to master with your head what you feel. That is the problem! The most important thing here is a sensation of not knowing what to do, to have your mind blank, or only scattered images that you cannot coordinate. It is a sensation of chaos. You are aware of what is going on but you can't control it. It is not like I am not aware that I was thinking stupid thoughts, but I was simply unable to stop thinking them (Salas & Yuen, 2016, p. 93)

This failure in Professor F's ego to inhibit negative mental representations is relevant in large part, as it shows how cognition shapes and manages feelings. Due to his dysexecutive impairment, every time he begins a new task or project, either at home or at his part-time job, he experiences a new crisis. In those moments, he struggles to make sense of what he is feeling on his own, and those negative feelings can linger for days:

> Having difficulties walking is something that saddens me. But then I have this experience that . . . well . . . I know it's OK to feel sad, but this is not just feeling sad, this is like a sticky sadness, which makes me feel sadder than I should. That is really, it is like when you step in the mud . . . so you need to make an effort to lift your foot, and in order to lift your foot you have to clean it too. I can't get out of the mud by myself . . . it's not a matter of intensity here, but the sensation of a weight, of mud, of something that grabs your foot. I'm afraid of the mud, because it is so sticky that even my capacity to imagine collapses. (Salas et al., 2014, pp. 318–319)

During the years, Professor F has developed several compensatory mechanisms to manage these recurrent crises. If we consider Goldstein's ideas on the relevance of how patients accommodate deficits, or manage to accomplish a task by using alternative routes, the logic behind these compensatory mechanisms is extremely important to understand. Since Professor F struggles to regulate negative feelings on his own, inside his head, he has begun to talk to others (both his therapist and his wife) and to write down his thoughts, as main compensatory strategies. It appears that such strategies facilitate verbal thinking by concretely placing thoughts outside his head, so they can be perceived either auditorily (listening to himself when talking to others and listening to how others rephrase what he says) or visually (reading). In both cases, Professor F appears to rely on the externalisation of verbal thinking as a mean to make sense of feelings and situations. Writing is a good example to illustrate the underlying compensatory mechanisms:

> Writing is like putting words to the mess. If I don't write everything goes to hell. If I think about it, but don't write it, it goes away . . . To think about ideas does not have the same effect, or the same order. I can't think. And if you ask me about repeating something . . . it is gone. This is how I work now, and it does not embarrass me to forget things. Writing helps me to put order in what I want to say, otherwise, I can't repeat it inside my head. It becomes something imperceptible, like waiting for words I do not have. It is as if I were blind, but conceptually blind. When I write it is like things emerge . . . and when I write I can return to those things. If I don't write it is like there is nothing inside my head, or sometimes only the feeling that there was something. But when I try to find what was there and I can't do it—that makes me feel anxious and powerless. (Salas & Yuen, 2016, p. 94)

It has been noted above that a psychoanalytic perspective to study depth psychological changes after brain damage does not only offer an opportunity to understand how patients' inner world has been modified by the injury (in the Freudian sense), but also how their capacity to relate to *other* minds has changed (in the relational sense). The case of Professor F offers numerous examples on this regard. However, the most remarkable change observed is a shift from intrinsic to extrinsic forms of emotion regulation when managing negative feelings (Salas et al., 2014). As has been described before, Professor F

struggles to use intrinsic emotion regulation strategies, such as changing the focus of attention to less negative contents (distraction), or
reinterpreting negative events in a more positive fashion (reappraisal).
In order to accommodate these problems, he has begun to rely on the
minds of others as a source of regulation, and it is through the use of
their minds that he is able to regain mental flexibility and reclaim his
thinking as a regulatory tool. He describes this phenomenon in relation to his wife, who helps him by offering questions in moments of
emotional turmoil:

> To ask me questions, questions that unfold me . . . questions that allow
> me to reflect upon me, to see myself. It is like putting it out there so
> you can see it as an image. My wife asks me, "Why are you sad? What
> happened to you?" She asks me questions, and those questions help
> me to put what I'm feeling out and think about it. It is a form of
> putting my head in order. There is something cognitive there . . . the
> fact that there is another possible way of arranging the same pieces.
> And by rearranging them you can breathe. I can't do that by myself.
> (Salas et al., 2014, pp. 318–319)

The use of the minds of others, as a source of emotion regulation,
can also be observed in relation to the therapist. Here, however,
extrinsic regulatory processes are more difficult to investigate, since
therapist and patient are usually immersed in regulatory interactions
during sessions, and most of the time they are unaware of its occur-
rence. The *a posteriori* reconstruction of these regulatory exchanges by
the therapist, in terms of how her mind becomes engaged with the
mind of the patient during different moments of a session, can offer
valuable information on this regard.

Allow us to illustrate this point with an example from Professor F's
case, where the therapist noted that his mind became regularly
engaged in "fantasy scaffolding" (Salas, 2012). As has been described
before, one of the core deficits in Professor F was a decrease in mental
generation, or stimulus-independent thinking. In other words,
Professor F's mind, when not reacting to external reality, tended to
become empty of contents, or what he described as the "blank mind".
This has important consequences for psychoanalytic technique, since
this method relies on patients reporting to the therapist their flux of
mental contents or fantasies, which are the raw material for analytic
work. In the case of Professor F, this flux was disrupted by recurrent

"internal silences". As a consequence, the therapist became progressively more aware of his own_fantasies, and how they emerged in response to Professor F's associations. He also began to systematically offer these fantasies to Professor F as material for joint exploration. Consider this reconstruction made by the therapist after a session (Salas, 2012):

> One day, during the period of returning to work after the accident, Professor F arrived to session commenting how much he disliked being at his office and that he did not know why, but he simply felt restless. He associated this with difficulties using the stairs to get to the first floor—his office was on the ground floor. When asked about the first floor he said: "Everything happens upstairs, most of the people from the department work there and usually share a cup of coffee during the breaks." At that point, two ideas came to the therapist's mind. First, he remembered how much Professor F enjoyed being with other people. Then a football field appeared as an image (Professor F was a football fan), and the thought of watching a football game from the sideline. So the therapist offered such fantasy to him by saying: "I was listening to you and an image of a football pitch came to my mind, and of someone watching a game from the sideline. Perhaps this is related to how you feel now returning to work." Professor F smiled and said "Yes, something like that." However, although he was smiling, the therapist noticed a subtle change in his own mood and started to feel melancholic. So he told him, "Now, when we are talking about this, I feel a little bit sad. I know that you told me you felt restless and uncomfortable in your office, but I wonder if it is because you feel sad in there."

Professor F's reliance on the therapist's fantasies, as a way of compensating for his difficulty in generating internal associations, can be considered a form of extrinsic regulation, where an external agent uses his own mental processes and contents to facilitate the regulation of negative feelings in others. In this case, the therapist used his own symbolic ability, by tuning it to the patient's emotional experience, and, thus, helping him to shape a rather somatic and undifferentiated emotional state (restlessness). This approach to understanding extrinsic emotion regulation when working with brain-injured patients is rooted in classic (alpha-function, Bion, 1963) and modern (mentalization, Fonagy et al., 2004; symbolisation, Freedman et al., 2011) psychoanalytic concepts. (For a detailed discussion on the potential uses of the concept of mentalization with this population, see Salas, 2012.)

Depending on the profile of cognitive impairment of each patient, different aspects of the therapist's mind (or the therapist's psychological abilities) can be recruited (Salas, 2008). In the case of Professor F, the therapist also reported that his mind became frequently engaged in several important tasks: linking somatic states with verbal representations, linking present and past experiences and facilitating the generation of narratives. Interestingly, Professor F was impaired in performing all these on his own. We believe that by adopting this relational approach it is possible to understand how damage to a particular brain area, and the associated impairment of a specific neuropsychological component, can change the way in which the mind of the patient relates to other minds. This "relational" point of view complements insight from observations of how the "inner" aspect of mental life can change after brain damage.

Some closing notes

The goal of this chapter was to provide the reader with a flavour of what a neuropsychoanalytic case looks like, by linking the subjective experience of deficits caused by brain injury and the neuropsychological components impaired by the damage to a specific brain area. Using the case of Professor F, we hope that the reader has been able to appreciate how, by correlating first- and third-person sources of information, a far richer and more dynamic picture of the brain–mind relationship emerges. In this case, such an approach offers novel insights into the potential role of the left dorso-medial PFC, and its associated cognitive operations, in supporting depth psychological processes such as intrinsic and extrinsic forms of emotion regulation.

In this chapter, we have attempted to summarise the methodological advances and importance of the case study approach in neuropsychology and neuropsychoanalysis, while emphasising that is far from being the only tool needed in the development of a coherent account of the mind–brain. We have also offered evidence to demonstrate that this approach is of special importance when exploring emotional and motivational aspects of the mind, by virtue of its appropriateness in capturing its subjective aspect, or the "view from within".

Neuropsychoanalysis, then, has much to offer to cognitive neuro-science, a field that has struggled to develop adequate theory and methodologies to study the sentient nature of the human brain. It is clear that, after brain damage, the emotional landscape of survivors changes. However, such changes cannot be reduced to individuals' performance of emotional tasks. This is far from sufficient, since emotion is perhaps the most ecological mental process of all. In this context, the psychoanalytic method, conceived as a "naturalistic setting" where the relationship of the self to others, and to itself, can be systematically observed and described, offers, no doubt, great opportunities.

The case of Professor F, we believe, also demonstrates that using a neuropsychoanalytic approach does not only offer theoretical advantages over purely cognitive approaches, but also is clinically useful. Neuropsychoanalytic observations occur in the context of a helping relationship, a working relationship that has facilitating emotional adjustment after the injury as a main goal. A better case formulation, one that considers not only cognitive variables, but also emotional ones, and, even more, one that acknowledges the dynamic interaction of cognitive and emotional elements, has a better chance to facilitate the process of accepting the changes brought about by brain damage. A neuropsychoanalytic view is, in conclusion, not only more accurate, but also very much more empathic with brain injury survivors and their strivings to preserve their identity.

Even though this chapter presents a very brief overview of a highly specialised field, we believe that some of the ideas presented here can be of special relevance for social workers. Social workers are key actors in the rehabilitation of individuals with many forms of neuro-logical disorders. They are often the first point of contact for patients in the community, and, in many cases, they become figures of emotional attachment and advice throughout patients' lives. Such a role is extremely challenging, since it requires the development of therapeutic skills in order to understand how a brain injury might have changed the way that a patient's mind works, as well as the way in which the patient now relates to others and himself. It is only through a profound knowledge of these elements that the development of a therapeutic alliance, and engagement with rehabilitation goals, is possible. The main idea proposed by this chapter is that, in order to respond these questions, first- and third-person perspectives need to be acknowledged, explored, and linked. For this purpose, it would be desirable for social workers to learn, through their training, a range of basic psychodynamic and neuropsychological skills, which can be used to facilitate the bridging of these two perspectives. The relevance of this task is not only theoretical or academic, in terms of gaining a better understanding of the neurological basis of mental processes, but also clinical. As we hope the case of Professor F illustrates, by understanding how brain damage can change inner experience (for example, the blank mind and the inability to self-regulate), we also acquire valuable knowledge as to how the difficulties that emerge from such changes can be therapeutically addressed (for example, an increased reliance on others as a source of regulation).

Notes

1. A list of key readings in psychodynamic neuroscience, clinical neuropsychoanalysis, clinical neuroscience, and history of neuropsychoanalysis can be found at https://npsa-association.org/education-training/suggested-reading/.
2. This "process focused" approach heavily influenced the work of modern neuropsychologists and is commonly known as The Boston Process Approach (Kaplan, 1988; Libon et al., 2013).
3. In the neuroses (e.g., hysteria; neurasthenia), no demonstrable lesion of the nervous system could be found at autopsy to account for the clinical symptomatology (e.g., paralysis, blindness) observed in the patient, thus impeding the relation of symptoms to damage to the brain.
4. In the 2016 meeting of the British Neuropsychological Society, a John Marshall Debate was held in order to discuss the following motion: "Human lesion neuropsychology will inevitably be replaced by neuroimaging as a research tool for understanding cognition". A vote count before and after the debate was 3:1 against the motion.
5. The distinction between psychoanalysis and psychoanalytic psychotherapy has been a focus of heated debate (see, for reviews, Fosshage, 1997; Joannidis, 2006; Kernberg, 1999). For the purpose of this chapter, we propose that "classic" psychoanalysis requires the consistent application of several "parameters", such as the use of free association and regular fifty minute sessions that take place several times a week. Psychoanalytic psychotherapy, in contrast, refers to the use of similar psychoanalytic concepts—unconscious processes,

transference–countertransference—but with a more flexible consideration of parameters.

6. Varela and Shear appear to use here the meaning of the word "eccentric" which, in Latin, has a spatial connotation (ekkentros = ek "out of" + kentron "centre"), and is commonly used to denote a circle, or orbit, that is not centred on the same point as another.

7. We are using the term "preconscious" in the way that Freud used it in his topographical model (Freud, 1915e), since it has direct links to the use of verbal representations in the regulation of emotion. To him, the preconscious system had a mediator role between unconscious contents and their coming to conscious awareness. More importantly, of all three systems, the preconscious had a particular relationship with language, for in this system is where word-presentations are attached to unconscious contents.

References

Anderson, S., & Tranel, D. (2002). Neuropsychological consequences of dysfunction in human dorsolateral prefrontal cortex. In: J. Grafman (Ed.), *Handbook of Neuropsychology* (pp. 145–156). Amsterdam: Elsevier.

Babinski, J. (1914). Contribution to the study of mental disorders in organic cerebral hemiplegia (anosognosia). *Revue Neurologique (Paris)*, 27: 845–848.

Beebe, B., & Lachmann, F. (2003). The relational turn in psychoanalysis: a dyadic systems view from infant research. *Contemporary Psychoanalysis*, 39(3): 379–409.

Ben-Yishai, Y., & Diller, L. (2011). *Handbook of Holistic Neuropsychological Rehabilitation*. New York: Oxford University Press.

Bion, W. R. (1963). *Elements of Psychoanalysis*. London: Karnac.

Bowen, C., Yeates, G., & Palmer, S. (2010). *A Relational Approach to Rehabilitation: Thinking about Relationships after Brain Injury*. London: Karnac.

Brain, W. R. (1941). Visual disorientation with special reference to lesions of the right hemisphere. *Brain*, 64: 224–272.

Carlsson, E., Paterson, B. L., Scott-Findlay, S., Ehnfors, M., & Ehrenberg, A. (2007). Methodological issues in interviews involving people with communication impairments after acquired brain damage. *Qualitative Health Research*, 17(10): 1361–1371.

Catani, M., Dell'Acqua, F., Bizzi, A., Forkel, S. J., Williams, S. C., Simmons, A., Declan, M., & Tiebauth de Schotten, M. (2012). Beyond cortical localization in clinico-anatomical correlation. *Cortex, 48*(10): 1262–1287.

Code, C. (1996). Classic cases: ancient and modern milestones in the development of neuropsychological science. In: C. Code, C.-W. Wallesch, Y. Joanette, & A. Lecours (Eds.), *Classic Cases in Neuropsychology* (pp. 1–10). Hove: Psychology Press.

Cory, G. A., & Gardner, R. (Eds.) (2002). *The Evolutionary Neuroethology of Paul MacLean: Convergences and Frontiers.* Santa Barbara, CA: Greenwood.

Cromwell, H. C., & Panksepp, J. (2011). Rethinking the cognitive revolution from a neural perspective: how overuse/misuse of the term "cognition" and the neglect of affective controls in behavioral neuroscience could be delaying progress in understanding the brainmind. *Neuroscience and Biobehavioral Reviews, 35*(9): 2026–2035.

Damasio, A. (2012). *Self Comes to Mind: Constructing the Conscious Brain.* New York: Vintage.

Evans, J. J., Gast, D. L., Perdices, M., & Manolov, R. (2014). Single case experimental designs: introduction to a special issue of *Neuropsychological Rehabilitation. Neuropsychological Rehabilitation, 24*(3–4): 305–314.

Feinberg, T., & Farah, M. (2000). A historical perspective on cognitive neuroscience. In: T. E. Feinberg & M. J. Farah (Eds.), *Patients Based Approaches to Cognitive Neuroscience* (pp. 3–20). Massachusetts: MIT Press.

Flyvbjerg, B. (2006). Five misunderstandings about case-study research. *Qualitative Inquiry, 12*(2): 219–245.

Fonagy, P., Gergely, G., Jurist, E., & Target, M. (2004). *Affect Regulation, Mentalization, and the Development of the Self.* London: Karnac.

Fosshage, J. L. (1997). Psychoanalysis and psychoanalytic psychotherapy: is there a meaningful distinction in the process? *Psychoanalytic Psychology, 14*(3): 409–425.

Fotopoulou, A., Pfaff, D., & Conway, M. A. (2012). *From the Couch to the Lab: Trends in Psychodynamic Neuroscience.* Oxford: Oxford University Press.

Freed, P. (2002). Meeting of the minds: ego reintegration after traumatic brain injury. *Bulletin of the Menninger Clinic, 66*(1): 61–78.

Freedman, N., Ward, R., & Webster, J. (2011). Towards a psychoanalytic definition of symbolization and desymbolization. In: N. Freedman, M. Hurvich, R. Ward, J. Geller, & J. Hoffenberg (Eds.), *Another Kind of Evidence. Studies on Internalization, Annihilation Anxiety, and Progressive Symbolization in the Psychoanalytic Process* (pp. 309–321). London: Karnac.

Freud, S. (1915e). The unconscious. *S. E., 14*: 159–204. London: Hogarth.

Gerstmann, J. (1940). The syndrome of finger agnosia, disorientation for right and left, agraphia and acalculia. *Archives of Neurology, Neurosurgery and Psychiatry, 44*: 398–408.

Goldstein, K. (1925/1971). Das Symptom, seine Entstehung und Bedeutung für unsere Auffassung vom Bau und von der Funktion des Nervensystems. In: A. Gurwitsch, E. Goldstein Haudek, & W. Haudek (Eds.), *Selected Papers/Ausgewählte Schriften* (pp. 126–153). Berlin: Springer (1971).

Goldstein, K. (1995). *The Organism: A Holistic Approach to Biology Derived from Pathological Data in Man.* New York: Zone Books.

Goodale, M. A., & Milner, A. D. (1992). Separate visual pathways for perception and action. *Trends in Neuroscience, 15*(1): 20–25.

Joannidis, C. (2006). Psychoanalysis and psychoanalytic psychotherapy. *Psychoanalytic Psychotherapy, 20*(1): 30–39.

Kächele, H., Schachter, J., & Thomä, H. (2009). *From Psychoanalytic Narrative to Empirical Single Case Research: Implications for Psychoanalytic Practice (Vol. 30).* New York: Taylor & Francis.

Kächele, H., Schachter, J., & Thomä, H. (2012). Single-case research: the German specimen case Amalia X. In: R. Levy, S. Ablon, & H. Kachele (Eds.), *Psychodynamic Psychotherapy Research* (pp. 471–486). New York: Humana Press.

Kaplan, E. (1988). A process approach to neuropsychological assessment. In: T. Boll & B. R. Bryant (Eds.), *Clinical Neuropsychology and Brain Function: Research, Measurement, and Practice: Master Lectures* (pp. 128–167). Washington, DC: American Psychological Association.

Kaplan-Solms, K., & Solms, M. (2000). *Clinical Studies in Neuropsychoanalysis.* London: Karnac.

Kernberg, O. F. (1999). Psychoanalysis, psychoanalytic psychotherapy and supportive psychotherapy: contemporary controversies. *International Journal of Psychoanalysis, 80*(6): 1075–1091.

Kolb, B., & Whishaw, I. Q. (2009). *Fundamentals of Human Neuropsychology.* London: Macmillan.

Lambon Ralph, M. A., Patterson, K., & Plaut, D. C. (2011). Finite case series or infinite single-case studies? Comments on "Case series investigations in cognitive neuropsychology" by Schwartz and Dell (2010). *Cognitive Neuropsychology, 28*(7): 466–474.

Leont'ev, A. N. (1981). The problem of activity in psychology. In: J. V. Wertsch (Ed. & Trans.), *The Concept of Activity in Soviet Psychology* (pp. 37–71). New York: Sharpe.

Libon, D. J., Swenson, R., Ashendorf, L., Bauer, R. M., & Bowers, D. (2013). Edith Kaplan and the Boston Process Approach. *Clinical Neuropsychologist, 27*(8): 1223–1233.

Liepmann, H. (1908). Die linke Hemisphäre und das Handeln. In: H. Liepmann (Ed.), *Drei Aufsätze aus dem Apraxiegebiet* (pp. 17–50). Berlin: Karger Publishers.

Luria, A. R. (1963). *Restoration of Function after Brain Injury*, B. Haigh (Trans.). Oxford: Pergamon Press.

Luria, A. R. (1966a). Kurt Goldstein and neuropsychology. *Neuropsychologia, 4*: 311–313.

Luria, A. R. (1966b). *Higher Cortical Functions in Man*. London: Tavistock.

Luria, A. R. (1968). *The Mind of a Mnemonist: A Little Book about a Vast Memory*. New York: Basic Books.

Luria, A. R. (1972). *The Man with a Shattered World: The History of a Brain Wound*. New York: Basic Books.

Luria, A. R. (1976). *The Working Brain: An Introduction to Neuropsychology*. New York: Basic Books.

Luria, A. R., & Majovski, L. V. (1977). Basic approaches used in American and Soviet clinical neuropsychology. *American Psychologist, 32*(11): 959.

McDonald, S. (2014). Facing the challenges of single-case experimental methodology. *Aphasiology, 29*(5): 575–580.

McNeil, J. E., & Warrington, E. K. (1993). Prosopagnosia: a face-specific disorder. *Quarterly Journal of Experimental Psychology, 46*(1): 1–10.

Milner, B., Corkin, S., & Teuber, H. L. (1968). Further analysis of the hippocampal amnesic syndrome: 14-year follow-up study of HM. *Neuropsychologia, 6*(3): 215–234.

Mitchell, S. (1988). *Relational Concepts in Psychoanalysis*. Cambridge, MA: Harvard University Press.

Nissen, T. & Wynn, R. (2014). The clinical case report: a review of its merits and limitations. *BMC Research Notes, 7*(1): 264–271.

Northoff, G., & Heinzel, A. (2006). First-person neuroscience: a new methodological approach for linking mental and neuronal states. *Philosophy, Ethics, and Humanities in Medicine: PEHM, 1*(1): 1–10.

Northoff, G., Bermpohl, F., Schoeneich, F., & Boeker, H. (2007). How does our brain constitute defense mechanisms? First-person neuroscience and psychoanalysis. *Psychotherapy and Psychosomatics, 76*(3): 141–153.

Panksepp, J. (1998). *Affective Neuroscience: The Foundations of Human and Animal Emotions*. New York: Oxford University Press.

Panksepp, J., & Solms, M. (2012). What is neuropsychoanalysis? Clinically relevant studies of the minded brain. *Trends in Cognitive Sciences, 16*(1): 6–8.

Paterson, B., & Scott-Findlay, S. (2002). Critical issues in interviewing people with traumatic brain injury. *Qualitative Health Research, 12*(3): 399–409.

Ramachandran, V. S. (Ed.) (2002). *Encyclopedia of the Human Brain* (Vol. 4). Cambridge: Academic Press.

Riese, W. (1959). *A History of Neurology*. New York: MD Publications.

Salas, C. E. (2008). Elementos relacionales en la rehabilitación de sobrevivientes de lesión cerebral adquirida. Alianza de trabajo, transferencia y contratransferencia, usos de terapeuta [Relational elements in the rehabilitation of brain injury survivors. Working alliance, transference and countertransference and therapist's uses]. *Revista Gaceta de Psiquiatría Universitaria*, 4(2): 214–220.

Salas, C. E. (2012). Surviving catastrophic reaction after brain injury: the use of self-regulation and self–other regulation. *Neuropsychoanalysis*, 14(1): 77–92.

Salas, C. E. (2014). Identity issues in neuropsychoanalysis. *Neuropsychoanalysis*, 16(2): 153–158.

Salas, C. E., & Yuen, K. S. L. (2016). Revisiting the left convexity hypothesis: changes in the mental apparatus after left dorso-medial prefrontal damage. *Neuropsychoanalysis*, 18(2): 85–100.

Salas, C. E., Radovic, D., Yuen, K. S. L., Yeates, G. N., Castro, O., & Turnbull, O. H. (2014). "Opening an emotional dimension in me": changes in emotional reactivity and emotion regulation in a case of executive impairment after left fronto-parietal damage. *Bulletin of the Menninger Clinic*, 78(4): 301–334.

Shallice, T. (1979). Case study approach in neuropsychological research. *Journal of Clinical and Experimental Neuropsychology*, 1(3): 183–211.

Shallice, T. (1988). *From Neuropsychology to Mental Structure*. Cambridge: Cambridge University Press.

Solms, M. (2000a). Preliminaries for an integration of psychoanalysis and neuroscience. *Annual of Psychoanalysis*, 28: 179–202.

Solms, M. (2000b). Freud, Luria and the clinical method. *Psychoanalysis and History*, 2(1): 76–109.

Solms, M., & Panksepp, J. (2012). The "Id" knows more than the "Ego" admits: neuropsychoanalytic and primal consciousness perspectives on the interface between affective and cognitive neuroscience. *Brain Sciences*, 2(2): 147–175.

Solms, M., & Saling, M. (1986). On psychoanalysis and neuroscience: Freud's attitude to the localizationist tradition. *International Journal of Psychoanalysis*, 67: 397–416.

Solms, M., & Turnbull, O. H. (2011). What is neuropsychoanalysis? *Neuro-Psychoanalysis*, 13(2): 133–145.

Stuss, D. T., & Alexander, M. P. (2007). Is there a dysexecutive syndrome? *Philosophical Transactions of the Royal Society of London. Series B, Biological Sciences, 362*(1481): 901–915.

Tate, R. L., Perdices, M., McDonald, S., Togher, L., & Rosenkoetter, U. (2014). The design, conduct and report of single-case research: resources to improve the quality of the neurorehabilitation literature. *Neuropsychological Rehabilitation, 24*(3–4): 315–331.

Turnbull, O. H. (2001). Cognitive neuropsychology comes of age. *Cortex, 37*(3): 445–450.

Turnbull, O. H., & Solms, M. (2004). Depth psychological consequences of brain damage. In: J. Panksepp (Ed.), *Textbook of Biological Psychiatry* (pp. 571–595). New Jersey: Wiley-Liss.

Vandenbroucke, J. P. (1999). Case reports in an evidence-based world. *Journal of the Royal Society of Medicine, 92*(4): 159–163.

Varela, F., & Shear, J. (1999a). *The View from Within. First-Person Approaches to the Study of Consciousness.* Thorverton: Imprint Academic.

Varela, F., & Shear, J. (1999b). First-person methodologies: what, why, how? In: F. Varela & J. Shear (Eds.), *The View from Within. First Person Approaches to the Study of Consciousness* (pp. 1–14). Thorverton: Imprint Academic.

Wachtel, P. (2008). *Relational Theory and the Practice of Psychotherapy.* New York: Guilford Press.

Wallerstein, R. (2002). The trajectory of psychoanalysis: a prognostication. *International Journal of Psychoanalysis, 83*: 1247–1267.

Wilson, B. (1999). *Case Studies in Neuropsychological Rehabilitation.* New York: Oxford University Press.

Wilson, B., & Gracey, F. (2010). Towards a comprehensive model of neuropsychological rehabilitation. In: B. Wilson, F. Gracey, J. Evans, & A. Bateman (Eds.), *Neuropsychological Rehabilitation* (pp. 1–21). New York: Cambridge University Press.

Wilson, B., Winegardner, J., & Ashworth, F. (2014). *Life after Brain Injury: Survivors' Stories.* Hove: Psychology Press.

Yeates, G. (2009). Posttraumatic stress disorder after traumatic brain injury and interpersonal relationships: contributions from object-relations perspectives. *Neuropsychoanalysis, 11*(2): 197–209.

Yeates, G. (2013). Towards the neuropsychological foundations of couples therapy following acquired brain injury (ABI): a review of empirical evidence and relevant concepts. *Neuro-Disability and Psychotherapy, 1*(1): 108–150.

PART II
IMPACT ON CLINICAL SESSIONS

CHAPTER FIVE

Psychoanalytic treatment of panic attacks: listening to the emotional system

Rosa Spagnolo

Schneider, in 2007, wrote, "In analytic work with certain types of patients manifesting panic states, words seem to have particularly little communicative value" (p. 1293); hence, our classical tools could not be efficient enough to promote the psychoanalytical process. If that is the case, we should make use of other analytic approaches to enable the therapeutic process. A way to enhance our understanding when "much of what is going on nonverbally is usually not talked about directly—it is simply experienced between the lines" (Herzog, 2011, p. 462), is to listen to, or feel, the patient's emotional life, by which means we might be able to reach the patient in his acute stage.

When the ability to think about a current situation is impaired, due to hyper-activation of the emotional systems, the acquisition of greater emotional control should be considered the first step in the development of the psychoanalytical process. During this development, we should follow the dreaming activity, since it shows us the changes in the patient's inner world (Fischmann, et al., 2013; Solms & Turnbull, 2002).

I shall describe the first phase of a psychoanalytic treatment of panic disorder (PD) (American Psychiatric Association, 1994, 2013) through clinical data of a female patient with severe fear and panic anxiety (PA),[1] intense bodily symptoms, sexual excitement, and strong arousal of executive functions.

Before introducing the topic, I shall report some work on the aetiology of panic disorder and then turn to Freud's libido and anxiety statements.

De Masi (2004), pursuing a useful integration of psychoanalysis and neuroscience, emphasises a mutual psychosomatic short-circuit between body and psyche, in which terror reinforces the somatic reactions and the psychic construction. He focuses on panic attacks as a consequence of the breakdown of the defence organisation at various levels. In this, he differentiates panic attacks from actual neuroses described by Freud.

Alexander and colleagues (2005) bring together Freudian psychoanalysis with classical conditioning and neurobiological research, as summarised by Blechner (2007):

> All these accounts of panic attacks refer to an increase in sensitivity of some alarm system. Klein's account suggests increased sensitivity of the suffocation alarm system. Gorman, LeDoux, and others suggest increased sensitivity of the fear network. Panksepp suggests increased sensitivity of the separation-distress system. What I am proposing is something different. I am proposing erratic inhibition and dissociation as additional important factors in panic attacks. The situation in the brain may be more erratic than hypersensitive. (p. 94)

Verhaeghe and colleagues (2007) argue that panic disorder, somatoform disorder, and undifferentiated somatoform disorder are three different manifestations of Freud's actual neurosis. Schneider (2007) also contributes in order to explore the underlying similarity in the psychic processes pertinent to both psychosomatic and panic disorders. Additional papers outline the lack of mentalization (Rudden et al., 2008) or symbolisation. Busch and colleagues (2009, 2010) suggest a series of potential interactions between brain, mind, environment, and efficacy of psychodynamic psychotherapy (Busch & Milrod, 2013).

There are different hypotheses from Panksepp and LeDoux, both of whom are important neuroscientists who sparked many studies on emotional systems.

LeDoux (2015) evokes the value of fear circuitry in panic aetiology. He considers the amygdala as an important component of limbic system, involved with the acquisition, storage, and expression of fear memory. In his work, "Coming to terms with fear" (2014), he gives reasons for different mechanisms of fear: conscious feeling and non-conscious process:

> We should reserve the term fear for its everyday or default meaning (the meaning that the term fear compels in all of us—the feeling of being afraid), and we should rename the procedure and brain process we now call fear conditioning. (p. 2874)

He suggests the name "defensive survival circuit", which is similar to what has been called a defence system (p. 2875).

These non-conscious system responses are elicited by threats and acted as conscious fear, in the panic attacks also.

Panksepp focuses on the SEEKING system (Panksepp, 2010; Panksepp & Biven, 2012) as a primal emotional system, outlining the involvement with the PANIC–GRIEF system (one of seven emotional systems) in the panic separation distress (Panksepp, 2005, 2011). At first he considered the SEEKING/DESIRE system (Alcaro, et al., 2007) to be a reward system that produced explorative energy; later, he studies its articulation with some psychiatric disorders (Panksepp & Watt, 2011; Zellner et al., 2011) and some specific psychoanalytic propositions such as libido, desire, and drive (Panksepp, 2011; Panksepp & Biven, 2012).

Currently, Wright and Panksepp (2012) consider that primal negative emotion, such as fear, panic, and rage, are able to inhibit the SEEKING system.

Libido and anxiety in Freud

In his early papers (Freud, 1893a, 1894a, 1895d), Freud suggests differentiating a form of conflictual anxiety named "psychoneuroses" from "actual neuroses" (phobia and panic) because the panic attack, therefore, would be non-conflictual, but simply linked to physio-pathological problems. This latter form could be derived from an accumulation of sexual desire that cannot be discharged: for instance, in those who abstain from normal sexual relationships. This excess of sexual tension, not experienced as sexual desire, would be a good trigger of anxiety. Initially, Freud (1896) linked the concept of libido to sexuality as a quantity of energy distinct from sexual arousal. Later, in the first topic, he separated object libido from ego libido (1905d, 1914c). The second topic is different.

While, in 1920, the ego held the role of containing the libido, in 1923, this role goes to the id, in order to neutralise the "clamour" produced by Eros. From this moment on, the vicissitudes of the libido follow that of Eros.

"What the Ego fears from or the danger posed by the libido in the Id cannot be determined; we know that the fear is of being over-whelmed or annihilated" (Freud, 1923b, p. 57).

In response to danger, the ego defends itself primarily through the release of anxiety. In this way, the ego controls the pleasure–unpleasure agency. However, by virtue of its bond with the external world, the ego also has a duty of ensuring survival and self-preservation, modulating the requests it receives from Eros, for its own safety and integrity.

Clinical presentation

Let us now turn to Giselle, a thirty-five-year-old woman, who decided to begin a psychoanalytic treatment after more than a year of cognitive–behavioural psychotherapy due to persistent symptoms of panic.

Giselle is a professional woman with an important, but not competitive, steady job; over the past twenty years, she has devoted her life to her husband and two sons. She got along with them and she wanted nothing else in her life.

Unexpectedly, during a short holiday, she meets and falls in love with a man who, in turn, also falls in love with her. Their reciprocated passion is so strong and satisfying that she begins to question all of her life's choices.

When she returns from this holiday, insomnia takes hold of her, leaving her unable to sleep at night. She feels like a trapped animal, with no way out. Every evening when she returns home after work, she experiences dizziness, shortness of breath, palpitations, sweating, and she wants to run away. She wants something, but she does not know exactly what, or where to find it. She is dominated by an instinct to seek something and a desire to escape. She wanders around aimlessly, looking for something, but she becomes upset and confused.

Giselle is restless. She would like to leave her husband, to move away, to get a different job. She no longer has any emotional contact with her sons. It seems as if she has lost all her previous modes of attachment. She immediately realises that something is wrong and she is scared. She feels lonely, trapped within her own wishes for change, and lost in an emotional world that overwhelms her with negative feelings.

Meeting her for the first time, she presented with a classic sequence of symptoms associated with panic disorder (Craske et al., 2010; Wittchen et al., 2010). At the beginning, they occurred only within the family unit, but soon they extended to other situations, such as during her job and daily life.

During our first sessions, she seemed frightened, scared, anxious ("Schreck, Furcht und Angst", Freud, 1920), expectant and incapable of concluding what she was saying.

Giselle seeks my help to find relief. She enquires and wants a reply. She needs me to be attuned to her because the slightest deviation throws her into turmoil and increases her feelings of loneliness and her wish to escape.

Her first dream:

> Our oldest friends were sitting at one table, while my husband and I sat at another one, alone. Our current friends were sitting at a third table. We were in a beautiful restaurant and everybody was ignoring each other, even though they knew each other. I tried and tried again to convince my husband to put everyone at one table, but he refused. I accepted his decision, though my great desire was to have all of us around the same table. I escaped from the room through narrows stairs to go upstairs. I found myself locked with him in a gloomy room. The dream now becomes black and white.

The few associations evoked by this dream revolve around the strict division of her life into separate relationships and her affective dependency on her husband. She describes him as moody and angry not only because he knows about her love affair (she breaks this up immediately after the vacation) but, she said, because he needs to have everything under his control.

I try to say something, starting from her associations, but she stops me at once, overwhelmed by panic and fear. She tries to contain this overflow through phobic avoidance (Wittchen et al., 2010), as the dream showed us. I keep silent, thinking about her emotional surrender (Knight, 2007), which was working against new connections.

The onset of the panic attacks transforms the quality of her emotional life. The analysis is invested with libidinal waves, alternating with bursts of anguish without any clear link with the events.

From what she recounts to me (confusing descriptions of daily events) and her intense emotional arousal, I deduce that we cannot go beyond the simple exploration of everyday life.

To give an example: she keeps telling me about the vicissitudes related to domestic life (husband, children, job), but as soon as a memory comes up, she becomes agitated and moves to avoid these topics. My words are useless as a reconnection device in these instances; I can show this kind of functioning (i.e., avoidance, withdrawal, anxiety, etc.) only when it arises in the sessions.

Some years ago, Knight (2007) wrote, "It has been noted for a long time that the heart of the change process in the therapeutic relationship relies more on an emotional experience for the patient than intellectualization or interpretation" (p. 279).

In my opinion, that excess of uncontrollable libidinal energy alternating with panic attacks and phobic avoidance undermined and weakened the structure of the ego in its adaptation to reality, that is, in its ability to face the reality.

Let us follow the patient.

During the first year of analysis, she needs to "play the game" (using her metaphor) in the field of "daily events". She imagines herself in a field with a ball that should be kicked. Sometimes she says, "I'm going to pass the ball", when she feels close to getting a panic attack. Or, "I am not able to start the game, I have to go into the other's field and play his game," she asserts, spending the whole session talking about her husband or lover, without ever using the pronoun "I".

It is as if everything is happening outside her; inside there is just confusion and anxiety.

In these moments, Giselle oscillates between a claustrophilic holding (Fachinelli, 1983; Meltzer, 1992), as expressed in her dreams, and her wish to escape from claustrophobic situations. Usually, as soon as I am about to say something regarding her dreams, she becomes upset, because she perceives herself as a frightened rabbit without a burrow to take shelter in. She takes a break for a few minutes and recovers, saying sweetly, "Sorry, I didn't understand what you said, could you repeat?" Through these moments, we can share her feeling of easily falling prey to fear and panic.

> In this case anxiety expresses the pre-reflective perception of being invaded and overwhelmed by non-regulated affects. It had not been possible to take these affects to a level for working through, modulating, symbolically representing and translating into language. (Bastianini & Moccia, 2009, p. 143)

In my patient, this pre-reflective perception was visible in the body: indeed, we have experienced freezing, choking, dizziness, blushing, chills, sweating, trembling, shaking, or trouble breathing, and so on. According to Damasio (2010):

> Body and brain are engaged in a continuous interactive dance. Thoughts implemented in the brain can induce emotional states that are implemented in the body, while the body can change the brain's landscape and thus the substrate for thoughts. . . . A small alteration on the brain side of the system can have major consequences for the body state . . . likewise, a small change on the body side . . . can have a major effect on the mind once the change is mapped and perceived as acute pain. (p. 78)

"Where is the pain?" I wondered.

The emotional excess and the urgency to act (motor discharge) have been in the foreground for months, but her dreams have never been accompanied by anxiety. For example, this repetitive dream:

> I don't remember where I was; there were wide streets. I was walking fast, entering a lot of pubs, looking for my beloved. I ended up locked in a dark room, from which my husband forbade me to exit. Despite that, I felt good, I was calm and with the idea that maybe it's better to stay there.

She associates, as usual, some daily event related to her family *ménage*, and adds a fantasy: "I would like to retire to a desert island, without anyone; a little house on the top of some mountain would be good; a small window overlooking a beautiful landscape could be enough. The first day, I will water a flower, the second, another flower, and the third, I will add yet another flower."

This association allows us to talk about our three sessions, her three sisters, and her strong claustrophilic call. I wonder about the window: it is the only opening in the house of her fantasy and I think to myself: "At least she did not close it! But she also wants to water the flowers and watch the scenery!"

Anyway, at that moment, I thought it was inappropriate to travel further into her memories. I did not know which ones could be traumatic and so I just showed her where we were on her dream map and I made a comment on this "opening–closing movement", like an "input or output" system experienced as pleasant or painful.

From avoidance to bewilderment via dream work

We have a vast literature on dreaming and its psychoanalytic impact. Just to summarise, in his interesting paper, "Consciousness: 'nothing happens unless first a dream'", Kessler (2013) observes—quoting Lakoff (1997)—that "the dream work exhibits the same type of figurative thinking that might produce metaphor, metonymy, conceptual blending, and irony in waking" (p. 179).

Blechner (2013) calls the choice of which of the dream's aspects the clinician and the dreamer focus on "vectors of interpretation", because "There may be more than one process in the instigation and construction of dreams" (p. 260).

Fosshage (2007, 2013) repeatedly stresses the value of this co-construction, to which both analyst and patient co-contribute, in order to maximise understanding.

I always ask my patients at first what they have felt throughout the dream and upon awakening and then, subsequently, whether they have even seen or felt something like that in their lives. This is meant to amplify the link between the narrative and the emotional world present in the dream (Blechner, 2001) and allows the partaking of this communication beyond the dream content.

HOTEL DREAM: I am at a hotel in bed with Y [the lover], A (her son) is in a small bed next to us. I think that I should not be seen with him, so I leave, passing from room to room, opening each door. There are sexual images projected on every wall and sexual scenes take place in every room. I cannot stand in the doorway, I could either enter, taking part, or go away. I escape, and, at the end of the corridor, there are my mother, my sisters, and an aunt of mine. I run away, I find my son again and we lock ourselves in a room.

After a moment of surprise at the "pornographic hotel dream", for which she seeks to find some link with her previous sexual life, she says, with a break in her voice, "In this dream, I encountered most of my relatives, except my husband." She slowly revisits the dream, passing through the corridor again and, as soon as she glimpses the female characters, she becomes scared (*"if they knew!"*, she exclaims) and adds a flash memory: in this dream, both her sons were sleeping wrapped up on the bedside table.

She processes this strange object by associating it with the necessity to divide her life into compartments (compartmentalisation, Meltzer 1992), in order to contain her anxiety within controllable boundaries. At this point, she recalls, unexpectedly, that inside her parent's bedroom there used to be a chest of drawers similar to the bedside table in the dream. The first drawer is locked. She becomes confused; she is not sure about this memory, maybe that drawer was used to change newborn babies or to contain their underwear. She is confused, but she goes on, asking herself what connection exists between the wild sexual scenes and her relatives. She gets into the "chiasma" (Chianese, 1994), which leads us to her insight: "If, in this dream, there had not been all those sex scenes, I could still think that I am a good mother, lover, daughter, who lives in three different rooms without passages to each other."

But that is not enough. She becomes confused and bewildered. I say nothing, I let the patient feel her confusion in the session.

Because I had not saturated the field with early interpretations, she is able to revisit this dream in several following sessions, in which she is looking for answers to her bewilderment.

This convinced me that a new path was open to us, because:

1. Here, there was a conjunction of quantity (the length of the dream, the richness of the images, the affects) with quality (the relationship's quality).

2.   The possibility of creating new records was apparent, without being pressed by fear and anxiety, relating new entries from the present to the past in order to reinforce new constructions.
3.   The hotel was more spacious compared to the small rooms featuring in the previous dreams, very populated and emotionally engaging (affect and object cathexis).

The richness of the dream's elements, linked to the condensation and figuration of dreams (Freud, 1900a), suggested that several circuits were now participating in its production. This was possibly a slight broadening of meaning, mapped on to the figuration of the dream, which pointed out possible routes in the variegated panorama of Giselle's mind.

> TOWN DREAM: I'm in a small town with my sisters; we are going to a party in C-town, to listen to a famous singer. We have taken a boat and are rowing out to sea. It is late at night. How can we get there—I am thinking—if they are on opposite sides, divided by a mountain, one mirroring the other? Slowly arriving, I am happy to see C-town, but, once out of the boat, everything looked the same, although it was not. I search the places known to me; everything seems the same, but it is not. I wake up, I feel a sense of bewilderment and, actually, I am still confused.

She associates, "The gate and a similar space, known, but unknown; also in that one [gate dream from the night before] the place was reached from a pathway, sometimes in the light, sometimes in the dark, as in this one." She wonders about the analytic paths, "Everything is the same as before, but different at the same time; as if some scenario is changing and I do not want that, I see it in a mirror."

This double perspective of mirroring that appears in her dreams makes me think about a "double register". I wonder, for a moment, about the activation of mirror neural networks, right and left brain hemispheres. Immediately, I come back to my analytic job: the double (mirror) image belongs to both the narcissism and the transference–countertransference that involves the analytic couple. By virtue of these reciprocal movements, some familiar elements might have been introduced (or reactivated): that is, the female analyst refers to a female axis identity (three sisters and mother), which has been transmitted from generation to generation.

We are now able to speak freely on this and when the fog (anxiety, confusion, and bewilderment) begins to dissolve, she can experience the feeling of separation, saying:

> Doctor, I never thought it was important to share this here; my father was unfaithful to my mother for decades, always with the same woman. During the day things were peaceful, but at night they fought. He packed his bags and she implored him not to do that. I usually stayed awake, listening to them and praying. He never left home. [She becomes emotional and cries.] My mother told us that staying with a man involved sacrifice and devotion. But I'm not like her and it makes me feel bad because I'm different from her and all my sisters.

From panic to pain

This highlights a long-lasting alliance between desire, pain, and separation. We share how her father, always unfaithful to his wife, unable or hesitant to end this relationship, forced on himself, as well as on his wife, the pain of an impossible separation: "Now I know that if emotions get out of hand, I erase everything, just as I wiped away my father in order to not get in touch with my mother's grief," she said.

In the following months, the quality of the narration surprises me, because it seems different from usual. There is an affective modulation in her account, not present earlier, that brings a different quality to her emotions.

I think about some of Matthis's reflections (2000) on affects and pain, and so I am trying to imagine a possible escape from those repetitive emotional circuits in order to be able to travel on new circuits when the unconscious steps in to help us (or, rather, the unconscious part of working through).

> CAVERN DREAM: I am in a cavern taking my high-school graduation exam and I do not understand anything. I try to ask for some help from people around me and I become anxious at seeing the others writing with ease. It is as if they are mumbling about something I cannot understand. Panic is approaching and I am still trying to find some answers, and so someone shows me a paper, but on it are written alien hieroglyphics. I don't understand. I run away and I chance upon my sister. I scream to her, asking for the answer, because I know that she has got it, but I can't

copy it, so I see X [her own husband], not so far away, coming towards me. I run to him for help, but he has a sneer that causes me anguish, so much so that I wake up, and now his face is really above my face and he's asking me questions. I do not understand and I cannot answer. He really has a sneer on his face, I am terrified and I feel that I could even die from that. Doctor, I dreamt "the panic", but it wasn't only a dream; when I woke up everything was true, the suffering was real.

Beyond the associations, this was certainly one of those dreams that turn a new page (Quinodoz, 2002), because it proposes a link between mind and body that seemed broken: it was not merely a dream, on waking up it was real, she said; the panic belonged to her mind, which could dream it, and to her body, which could feel it.

This new integration allows us to take a step further in the direction of emotional control.

First of all, she is thinking of herself as affected by panic attacks, and after that she starts to look for the passkey to affective codes (alien hieroglyphics), indecipherable up to now. Now it was clear that the emotions were, in fact, never confined to one place, but pervaded contiguous areas related to object differentiation/separation. This object that should have protected her for a long time from "Schreck, Furcht and Angst" was the same one who was questioning her with a sneer.

She regains control over herself and decides to separate from her husband.

After this dream, the panic attacks disappear. Giselle is always little restless, she looks for a new apartment to live with her sons. On the day of the move, just as she is on the threshold of her new home, she changes her mind and goes back to her husband. The day after, she says:

Doctor, I have an acute pain here [indicates her heart with her hand], and there are no words to explain it. I felt it yesterday when I did not have the strength to leave him. I felt a pang in my heart. It is a real pain; until you have lived it yourself, you cannot believe it. If I cannot face this pain, I will never get rid of it.

She stayed silent for a long time with her own pain.

I thought that the heart was the right place to feel this tolerable pain, now accessible for the psychoanalytic work.

Some closing remarks

How (in what form) infantile desire (unconscious codes) allows for deviation in the course of self-identification in order not to experience pain is the topic of current analysis (after about eighteen months).

The phantom of the primal scene (*Urszene*), charged with ambivalence, erotic relations in terms of perpetual sensory stimulation as well as secret retreats, have made their way (due to greater thinkability) into the analysis.

We started with an excess of libido and anxiety and, now, they no longer exist.

For the analytic work, in this acute stage, what Blechner (2007) writes is certainly true:

> [It] has reestablished dissociated links between cognitive content and affect. Psychoanalytic therapy can do both: extinguish inappropriate cognitive–affective links, and reestablish appropriate cognitive affective links, (p. 94)

However, I wonder, if we had not worked on the emergence of emotional dysregulation in order to establish new possible connections between past and present (new configurations), would we have been able to reach the perception of pain as a starting point for future psychoanalytic work?

We might conclude that, during this first part of therapy, the focus had been on anxiety, libidinal excess, and panic control (because they were strongly in the foreground). Getting into contact with the desire to separate from her husband triggered the panic attacks, and prevented her from attaining a sufficient level of lucidity to cope with the separation process. It has been necessary to follow her emotional heart, step by step, up to the point of intersection with the pain. The discovery that is possible to feel pain in both body and mind, as a feeling and also as something thinkable, has also been an important achievement for the psychoanalytic process. Dreams have assisted us on the journey we have taken together, revealing her unconscious functioning.

My sensible and careful consideration in listening to/feeling her emotional life supported me in gaining a better understanding of what was happening (in her current daily life and in the psychoanalytic field) and in finding the right timing for my interventions.

For me, it is not possible to determine which circuits were switched on/off by the psychoanalytic treatment (Boeker et al., 2013) in order to reach the level of emotional control, finally gained by the patient. I can hypothesise that, through the unconscious transference–countertransference movement, it was possible to activate some affects connected to early relationships that nurtured uncontrolled anxieties and fears. *Inter alia*, it was possible to reach these affective codes only after overcoming (deactivating) the panic circuit.

Following this path, we gained access to pain, due to the loss of love for the object (active movement of disinvestment) and, at the end, we arrived at the narcissistic reinvestment of the self through a work of lengthy sensory restoration (and reintegration) in the emotional space, which influences the shaping of feelings and enhances desire.

Note

1.   PAs are defined currently as a brief period of intense fear or discomfort in which four or more of a list of thirteen symptoms develop abruptly and reach a peak within ten minutes (Craske et al., 2010, p. 94).

References

Alcaro, A., Huber, R., & Panksepp, J. (2007). Behavioral functions of the mesolimbic dopaminergic system: an affective neuroethological perspective. *Brain Research Reviews, 56*: 283–321.

Alexander, B., Feigelson, S., & Gorman, J. M. (2005). Integrating the psychoanalytic and neurobiological views of panic disorder. *Neuropsychoanalysis, 7*: 129–141.

American Psychiatric Association (1994). *The Diagnostic and Statistical Manual of Mental Disorders* (4th edn) (*DSM-IV*). Arlington, VA: American Psychiatric Association.

American Psychiatric Association (2013). *The Diagnostic and Statistical Manual of Mental Disorders* (5th edn) (*DSM-V*). Arlington, VA: American Psychiatric Association.

Bastianini, T., & Moccia, G. (2009). Anxiety: a form of affect semiosis some theoretical–clinical reflections on panic pathologies. *Italian Psychoanalytic Annual, 3*: 137–152.

Blechner, M. J. (2001). *The Dream Frontier*. Hillsdale, NJ: Analytic Press.

Blechner, M. J. (2007). Approaches to panic attacks. *Neuropsychoanalysis, 9*: 91–100.

Blechner, M. J. (2013). New ways of conceptualizing and working with dreams. *Contemporary Psychoanalysis, 49*(2): 259–275.

Boeker, H., Richter, A., Himmighoffen, H., Ernst, J., Bohleber, L., Hofmann, E., Vetter, J., & Northoff, J. (2013). Essentials of psychoanalytic process and change: how can we investigate the neural effects of psychodynamic psychotherapy in individualized neuro-imaging? *Frontiers in Human Neuroscience, 7*: 355.

Busch, F. N., & Milrod, B. L. (2013). Panic-focused psychodynamic psychotherapy—extended range. *Psychoanalytic Inquiry, 33*: 584–594.

Busch, F. N., Milrod, B. L., & Sandberg, L. S. (2009). A study demonstrating efficacy of a psychoanalytic psychotherapy for panic disorder: implications for psychoanalytic research, theory, and practice. *Journal of the American Psychoanalytic Association, 57*: 131–148.

Busch, F. N., Oquendo, M. A., Sullivan, G. M., & Sandberg, L. S. (2010). An integrated model of panic disorder. *Neuropsychoanalysis, 12*: 67–79.

Chianese, D. (1994). Il chiasma. *Rivista Italiana di Psicoanalisi, 3*: 517–531.

Craske, M. G., Kircanski, K., Epstein, A., Wittchen, H. U., Pine, D. S., Lewis-Fernández, R., Hinton, D., Phillips, K., Hofmann, S., Klein, D., Klein, R., Rapee, R., & Stein, M. (2010). Panic disorder: a review of DSM-IV panic disorder and proposals for DSM-V. *Depression & Anxiety, 27*: 93–112.

Damasio, A. (2010). *Self Comes to Mind: Constructing the Conscious Brain*. New York: Pantheon.

De Masi, F. (2004). The psychodynamic of panic attacks: a useful integration of psychoanalysis and neuroscience. *International Journal of Psychoanalysis, 85*: 311–336.

Fachinelli, E. (1983). *Claustrofilia*. Milan: Adelphi.

Fischmann, T., Russ, M. O., & Leuzinger-Bohleber, M. (2013). Trauma, dream, and psychic change in psychoanalyses: a dialog between psychoanalysis and the neurosciences. *Frontiers in Human Neuroscience, 7*: 877 doi: 10.3389/fnhum.2013.00877.

Fosshage, J. L. (2007). The organizing functions of dreaming: pivotal issues in understanding and working with dreams. *International Forum of Psychoanalysis, 16*: 213–221.

Fosshage, J. L. (2013). The dream narrative: unconscious organizing activity context. *Contemporary Psychoanalysis, 49*(2): 253–258.

Freud, S. (1893a). On the psychical mechanism of hysterical phenomena: preliminary communication (with J. Breuer). *S. E., 2*: 1–17. London: Hogarth.

Freud, S. (1894a). The neuro-psychoses of defence. *S. E.*, *3*: 43–61. London: Hogarth.

Freud S. (with Breuer, J.) (1895d). *Studies on Hysteria*. *S. E.*, *2*. London: Hogarth.

Freud, S. (1896). The aetiology of hysteria. *S. E.*, *3*: 189–221. London: Hogarth.

Freud, S. (1900a). *The Interpretation of Dreams*. *S, E.*, *4–5*. London: Hogarth.

Freud, S. (1905d). *Three Essays on the Theory of Sexuality*. *S. E.*, *7*: 125–245. London: Hogarth.

Freud, S. (1914c). On narcissism. *S. E.*, *14*: 69–00. London: Hogarth.

Freud, S. (1920g). *Beyond the Pleasure Principle*. *S. E.*, *18*: 7–64. London: Hogarth.

Freud, S. (1923b). *The Ego and the Id*. *S. E.*, *19*: 3–66. London: Hogarth.

Freud, S. (1926d). *Inhibitions, Symptoms and Anxiety*. *S. E.*, *20*: 77–174. London: Hogarth.

Herzog, B. (2011). Procedural interpretation: a method of working between the lines in the nonverbal realm. *Psychoanalytic Inquiry*, *31*: 462–474.

Kessler, R. J. (2013). Consciousness: "nothing happens unless first a dream". *Contemporary Psychoanalysis*, *49*(2): 176–188.

Knight, Z. G. (2007). The analyst's emotional surrender. *Psychoanalytic Review*, *94*: 277–289.

Lakoff, G. (1997). How unconscious metaphorical thought shapes dreams. In: D. Stein (Ed.), *Cognitive Science and the Unconscious*. Washington, DC: American Psychiatric Press.

LeDoux, J. E. (2014). Coming to terms with fear. *PNAS*, *111*(8): 2871–2878.

LeDoux, J. E. (2015). *Anxious: Using the Brain to Understand and Treat Fear and Anxiety*. New York: Viking.

Matthis, I. (2000). Sketch for a metapsychology of affect. *International Journal of Psychoanalysis*, *81*: 215–227.

Meltzer, D. (1992). *The Claustrum. An Investigation of Claustrophobia*. Strathtay, Perthshire: Clunie Press.

Panksepp, J. (2005). Commentary on "integrating the psychoanalytic and neurobiological views of panic disorder". *Neuropsychoanalysis*, *7*: 145–150.

Panksepp, J. (2010). Affective neuroscience of the emotional brainmind: evolutionary perspectives and implications for understanding depression. *Dialogues in Clinical Neuroscience*, *12*: 533–545.

Panksepp, J. (2011). The "dynamic unconscious" may be experienced: can we discuss unconscious emotions when there are no adequate measures of affective change? *Neuropsychoanalysis*, *13*(1): 51–59.

Panksepp, J., & Biven, L. (2012). *The Archaeology of Mind: Neuroevolutionary Origins of Human Emotion.* New York: W. W. Norton.

Panksepp, J., & Watt, D. (2011). Why does depression hurt? Ancestral primary-process separation distress (PANIC/GRIEF) and diminished brain reward (SEEKING) processes in the genesis of depressive affect. *Psychiatry, 74*: 5–13.

Quinodoz, J. M. (2002). *Dreams That Turn Over a Page. Paradoxical Dreams in Psychoanalysis.* London: Routledge.

Rudden, M. G., Milrod, B., Aronson, A., & Target, M. (2008). Reflective functioning in panic disorder patients: clinical observations and research design. In: F. N., Bush (Ed.), *Mentalization: Theoretical Considerations, Research Findings, and Clinical Implications* (pp. 185–206). New York: Taylor & Francis.

Schneider, J. A. (2007). Panic as a form of foreclosed experience. *Psychoanalytic Quarterly, 76*: 1293–1316.

Solms, M., & Turnbull, O. H. (2002). *The Brain and the Inner World.* New York: Other Press.

Verhaeghe, P., Vanheule, S., & De Rick, A. (2007). Actual neurosis as the underlying psychic structure of panic disorder, somatization, and somatoform disorder: an integration of Freudian and attachment perspectives. *Psychoanalytic Quarterly, 76*: 1317–1350.

Wittchen, H. U., Gloster, A. T., Beesdo-Baum, K., Fava, G. A., & Craske, M. G. (2010). Agoraphobia: a review of the diagnostic classificatory position and criteria. *Depression & Anxiety, 27*: 113–133.

Wright, J. S., & Panksepp, J. (2012). An evolutionary framework to understand foraging, wanting, and desire: the neuropsychology of the seeking system. *Neuropsychoanalysis, 14*(1): 5–39.

Zellner, M. R., Watt, D. F., Solms, M., & Panksepp, J. (2011). Affective neuroscientific and neuropsychoanalytic approaches to two intractable psychiatric problems: why depression feels so bad and what addicts really want. *Neuroscience and Biobehavioral Reviews, 35*: 2000–2008.

CHAPTER SIX

What does a patient with a gambling addiction "really want"?

Tiziana Bastianini*

I n this chapter, I will try to highlight the way in which some traumatic conditions (see cumulative trauma, Khan, 1963) experienced early in life (neglect, psychological abuse, disinvestment) and sometimes misunderstood, allow us to understand the developmental processes underlying an experience of addiction. At the dawn of psychic life, meanings, be these traumatic or generative, cannot be thought. However, the experiences of early years of life become inscribed in our memory in various registers that affect our moods and our outlook on the world. With his theory of *après-coup*, Freud tells us that the child does not have the means to digest the impact of the emotions aroused by some events:

> Only later in life—in a kind of second coming—will stored affect be registered, often by attaching itself to a minor life experience. From our adolescence onwards we are therefore visited continually by arrivals from early lived experience. (Bollas, 2008, p. 99)

In other words, we should try to understand the complex relationship between early experiences, genetic inheritance, and adult psychopathology through considering "defensive auto-protections" and

* The author wishes to thank Valentina Livolsi for sharing the clinical material discussed in supervision and presented in this chapter.

creative elaborations a person might have carried out. In this chapter, we will attempt to illuminate the hidden question behind patient A's addiction.

A's history

A's parents separated when he was very young. His father left to build a new family with a woman with whom he later had two more children (roughly when A entered adolescence), whereas A and his younger brother (who was one year younger) stayed at home to be raised by their mother. The boys' relationship with their mother was very close, with few rules and boundaries: the mother slept with her children and "ran naked through the house", in an "incestuous" climate in which physical and psychic boundaries were very flimsy. In general, A described his mother as a woman who "never did anything she really liked and whose only 'source of life' were her children, whom she experienced as extensions of herself".

The mother acted with "narcissistic seduction", with the result of creating an identifying dynamic founded on her need to exclusively possess her children's mind (and her children's assimilative need to ensure the continuity and stability of this link). From this perspective, "narcissistic identification" colonised A's psyche.

During the treatment we will come to understand that the confusing maternal object dwelled entirely in A's psychic space, binding it to a form of persecutory experience. That controlled it from the inside and constantly emptied it of subjective sense. It was difficult for A to gain support from a maternal object that, at any time, was likely to take the form of a usurping, invading object, leaving him passive and helpless through domination.

A described himself as a child who kept no secrets from his mother. He confided to her in everything: "even about the joint I couldn't lie!" The parent, who was clearly unable to discern the generational difference and the limits related to it, bound the subject to an omnipotent defensive experience. When subjectivity is marked by forms of trespass, intrusion and defenses from assimilation, the self can fail to go through the vicissitudes of separation, in terms of both mourning and differentiation. In this situation, we are faced with traces of an object that has failed in its role of "container". For A, the period between secondary and high school was very difficult: his mother became ill with breast cancer and had to undergo very painful procedures. At the same time, A entered a group of peers "who became criminals": they engaged in petty theft, participated in a few fights and made occasional use of cocaine.

Between secondary school and college, A's best friend accused him of theft. Though A denounced this crime, he began high school with "the reputation of the thief everyone knew". A feeling of guilt and shame accompanied him at this time.

When A was fifteen years old, his mother's cancer entered remission. She decided to move to Tunisia to start a business and finally take up a job she liked. With that decision, the mother created A's experience of abandonment, and he felt she had disrupted his life by turning his universe upside-down: "for me, doctor, it was impossible and instead was happening [. . .] after that, I thought nothing could happen to me [. . .] I didn't care and also put myself at risk".

At this time, A's father took the decision to bring A and his brother to live with his new family. This heralded a terrible time for A, who was coping with both the abandonment of his mother as well as obligation to live with his father. He found difficult to confront a father figure he failed to recognise as an authority, because the father had not been present in his childhood except "to punish us". He experienced great sorrow mixed with anger, but he could not share this with his mother, who "burst into tears just when I tried to talk and then my anger increased". At the same time, he learnt to defend himself through a progressive emotional freezing. As he reported in the second meeting: "there are things walled up inside me".

> If, in the fantasy of early growth, there is contained death, then at adolescence there is contained murder. [. . .] growing up means taking the parent's place. It really does. In the unconscious fantasy, growing up is inherently an aggressive act. (Winnicott, 1971, p. 195)

The child is motivated to "kill in security" the "sacred bond", in order to address the process of self-seeking through the biological and psychic transformations encountered at the end of latency. In doing so, the child creates new organisations of the psychical structures that are particularly significant in the evolutionary sense, as well as unconscious constraints on the "psychic solutions" previously achieved. The adolescent's experience is influenced by puberty, which leads him or her to break away from infantile idealisations and the omnipotence of thought in order to embrace sexuality and the ability to reproduce. Nevertheless, such experiences (and their effects on thought) are affected by intersubjective exchanges in early childhood, as manifested through psychic structures and emotional regulation.

When A was seventeen years old, during New Year's celebrations, he saw for the first time his father playing poker. Thus began his relationship with the game (imitation and the oedipal challenge are the psychic tracks by which the patient made sense of his relationship with his father). A began to play and win: the game gave him a sense of excitement, an adrenalin charge, and money.

A was rejected in high school, but he did not care: he decided to pay for private school himself and, in this way, he said: "I kicked my father out, because, at that point, I was paying for my education, and he couldn't tell me anything". A decided to leave his then-girlfriend (L) and dedicate himself to improving in poker game. He entered different clubs and, at the same time, played a lot online, often playing all night. This altered his sleep-wake cycle, as well as his eating habits, and he gained fifteen kilos. With girls, he had casual sex with no involvement, since, when he felt involved, he could not continue the relationship. On a couple of occasions, he engaged with prostitutes, though the memories of these experiences mortified him. The "bubble" of poker seemed to own him completely, in an addiction that remained neither conceivable nor nameable for a long time.

For a couple of years, he played professionally and he even gained a sponsor. He reconciled with his high school girlfriend (L) who, over time, began to question whether he was "playing too much, changing personality when playing, not having interest and time for other things". L, who had previously been in treatment at the university clinic, ultimately directed A to the practice.

When A came to the clinic, he was twenty-two years old and his defensive structure was beginning to waver: this made poker a particularly delicate subject to speak about. It was a complex defensive strategy for him and, at the same time, "It's my job, the only thing I can do, I'm good at [. . .] outside I have nothing". For A, poker was a defensive strategy through which he had learned to "adjust" his affective states.

From a symptomatic point of view, as emerged during psychotherapy, A frequently experienced moments of emptiness and emotional dissociation through which "I become like a plant, I don't exist, I do not feel anything". The alarming sensation of having to run away from the world and from himself was one of the profound motivations that led him to seek psychotherapeutic help.

Reflections on A

By the end of the very first meeting, A was able to ask for help, revealing his fears and asking for an appointment just before one of his next departures.

His therapist described him, at the age of twenty-two, as an apparently "well-off" boy; he often appeared bored and impatient with respect to some of the practice rules. He did not present as a "classic" compulsive gambler: although he showed some escalations in his need to re-play every time he lost, he also kept some savings secure, at the same time. Money seemed to serve the function of denying him any kind of addiction and simultaneously keeping alive his illusion of self-sufficiency—of being able to "self-sustain himself".

On the other hand, it also appeared to be his only mean of combating his perceived lack of value: "in reality, doctor, I have nothing [. . .] only a certificate that I bought in a private school!"

It was possible to link these communications to A's pervasive and omnipotent phantasy to one day "win a million euros" in order to do, without limits, whatever he wanted. This omnipotent phantasy, repeatedly revived, seemed to serve as an answer to the pain of loss. In fact, a melancholic core pervaded A's experiences; this was an off-psychic, devitalised, void core, emptied of any desire or even energy for desire. In A's stories, his girlfriend always proposed that they do something together; he would indulge her, but he described himself as "apathetic and always a bit elsewhere [. . .] often tired".

A's unconscious "pact with the devil" allowed him to avoid the pain of losing the object, though this condemned him to make no life experiences, detaching him from all ties with the outside world (Freud, 1915b; Ogden, 2005).

A also referred to frequent periods of low sexual desire and long moments spent lying in bed, watching TV shows or sleeping through almost all of the daylight hours. The depressive void inside him, leaving him feeling psychically dead, pushed A to evoke emotional responses in the therapist in order to feel psychically alive. "I play poker to live", he kept repeating. For many sessions the therapist felt pulled into a psychic mêlée that turned around a single point: A wanted to convince her that poker was only his work and that there was nothing else, but there was only "the poker" in his life.

A "guardian self" struggled to preserve his vital refuge. Without that self, he would have to deal with the pain of loss, expose himself to the risk of becoming emotionally dependent and meet catastrophic emotional states (here, I will not take into account the related technical problems inherent in treating those areas of mental functioning).

The therapist often described A as a patient who could elicit her pity. He would accuse her of negatively influencing his relationship with poker and making him a loser—just as his girlfriend L also did. A seemed to derive a sense of wellbeing from projecting his affective states outside his self. He was skilled at voicing helplessness to escape from what troubled him, repeating to his therapist: "this is the only thing I have and you want to take it off me!" A viewed his therapist as an annihilating object, ready to humiliate him and render him passive—a woman who took away his vital refuge.

The therapist perceived A's helplessness and frustration. She also perceived, despite his defensive armour, a sensitive boy with some resources (perhaps those that had initially led him to seek help, in the hopes for a different future). She saw him as completely turned into himself and absorbed by his attempt to not "lose" the desire and ability to play poker, as if there was no chance for him to feel alive.

However, A also felt another part of himself—a part that he needed help to navigate and one with which he engaged in grueling confrontations. This part of himself ruled the presence–absence rhythm in the sessions, according to his manner of controlling every experience of potential emotional dependency. A countertransferential fear of hurting A or asking "too much" was quietly understood by the therapist as a projective identification of the patient's similar feeling to be able to damage his loved objects. A very often felt guilty towards people he loved (his brother, his girlfriend) and showed impatience when the therapist tried to propose an understanding that departed from the iron logic of his archaic superego. He felt especially guilty about his relationship with his mother, for whom he could feel "nothing, but anger and discomfort [. . .] I feel like a bad son". The feelings of guilt and anger seemed to condense into a representation of the self as destructive to the other; painful affections were similar to the self (bad).

A, in the memories he recalled, evoked a frail and depressive mother, who could make him feel that any expression of his own needs was something that could involve her in a kind of unsustainable psychical experience. The patient internalised everything as unacceptable, selfish or "unfair", and potentially harmful to the object.

The affection that did not receive the "contingent response of the object" in the formative years of his childhood was perceived as potentially harmful, and subsequently dissociated.

Besides this representation of himself as guilty, as therapy progressed, an image of himself as "small and helpless" emerged. A's preadolescent phantasy was that he had a small penis—smaller than others' (not differentiating from the mother meant having a small penis). Therefore, he would not allow himself to reveal his body among peers in the football locker room.

This phantasy was also related to his representation of a totally undervalued father: a father who, in A's childhood, when he was immersed in the maternal claustrum, existed only to administer physical abuse. A father, also, that the teenager A had been able to subdue and overthrow, triumphing over him, and with whom he shared exclusively a few dark moments: the two of them sitting on the couch for hours, sometimes at night, "staring at the screen", without being able to sleep, and, at the same time, without speaking.

The father had racked up failures and played poker, but never became "really good, as I did". From this point of view, even the patient's aggressive part seems not to have found containment, rules or thinking. In other words, an object capable of establishing limits. Rather, A struggled, and ultimately failed, to differentiate from his mother, with whom he primarily identified, and did not host any traces of his father in his mind.

A's frequent opposition to his therapist's interpretations was also a transference communication in relation to an internal object that could invade him at any time and that he had to attack, thus feeling guilty. Gradually, it became possible for him to begin to think about poker as a tool that—in addition to being his job!—gave him back strong emotions and a sense of self-efficacy, which was so important for him.

Only with the passage of time it was possible to speak about the part played by chance and unpredictability in the game, which he felt he could only partially take under control. He found being at the mercy of winning/losing less painful or frightening than feeling emotionally dependent on someone: such dependence was deeply feared, though this fear had been long denied or dissociated. The fear had also been solicited by the therapeutic experience, in the transference and A's emotional rapprochement to L.

Often, A tried to manipulate the setting; he was sometimes aggressive, sometimes quite dismissive and sometimes failed to inform the therapist if was going to miss a session, making her feel at the mercy of his discontinuous investment. In a particularly emotionally significant session, when A had just discovered his mother's serious physical condition, he was, for once, able to show his pain, crying with despair, wearing his sunglasses, and then finally taking them off.

The patient's emotional involvement strongly emerged when he decided to live in London. It was very hard for him to talk about his departure, he was afraid of being manipulated by the therapist. He refrained from commenting on London and angrily denied any emotions inherent in moving away from the treatment, in a sort of flight from the opportunity to think about his pain. In his words: "I will ignore it, until the end".

I conclude with the therapist's words: "I left him with the feeling that we had made a good grounding for more work. Meanwhile, I understood that it was impossible for him to stay in Rome with his mother, and perhaps also with me in the transference. Just as he had begun to be able to show and share his pain, the recurrence of his mother's cancer, so aggressive and 'terminal', had reactivated attachments and rekindled emotions that were too painful and violent. He is leaving Rome, I thought, to recover within himself a little of his vital elements".

I would like to conclude this chapter with clinical notes showing the work done during psychotherapeutic treatment, psychodynamically oriented.

Dreams

A had two dreams:

> One tonight which I didn't write, the other a few nights ago and I wrote it here—holding the phone—I don't remember very well that of tonight.
>
> I am in a café with two of my friends (I think one is from the time of the pool) and, at another table, there were two girls (of the past, perhaps school time?).
>
> At some point I get a text message saying "An Italian is lost in Barcelona". We went down the stairs to leave the place and at the door I met my

best friend [Sara] from secondary school. She sees me and I say: "You know who I am?" She says "No". I say "I am A", then she jumps on me and gives me a kiss on the cheek, which takes about 5 minutes.

[T = Therapist; P = Patient]

T: What comes to your mind?

P: I don't know . . . it's a very strange dream. There are people I didn't expect, so it seems strange. And then I don't understand what they may have in common . . .

T: I could think they are people of the past, for example Sara, your best friend at secondary school, recalls a time away. As if in these dreams there is a look at A of the past . . . a different guy from who you are today.

P: He tells me something about male characters, who are not from the past, then says "Female characters yes".

T: Last time you also talked about the fact you used to be a different guy.

P: Yes, yes emotionally, I was another person. With Sara we spent a lot of time together and shared many experiences, but after secondary school I haven't seen or heard about her. [. . .] See, sometimes I think about reactions that I should have to certain things, then I look at my true reaction and practically there are no reactions. I am like a robot standing there and don't react to anything. How do you live this way? I think it is bad . . .

T: As if nothing could touch you . . .

P: Yes, I don't like to depend on the others. Let's say as just as I feel I may have a different relationship with someone, a little more emotional, I feel stuck. I cannot make it. I feel like frozen. And I have to keep checking on the other person, even the smallest thing, phrases and words. I miss the beautiful things in life. What is life if you don't get emotional?

In the dream, you might think the Italian who "got lost" is the patient, who feels he has missed out because of his dissociative defenses against the pain of growing at the beginning of adolescence (Do you recognise me?). However, these attempts to avoid grief, loss and separation came at the huge cost of sacrificing the very source of A's emotional life. The crisis that was caused by his lack of sense of self early in his developmental processes introduced him to confusion, vulnerability and dependence on external figures to organise and regulate his own development.

Session 23: 11 November 2013

From May, A and the therapist met twice per week. A few days before this session, A's mother had been hospitalised for some checks; her condition was unknown.

A spoke of his friend Chiara, who went with him to see his mother at the hospital. Chiara had told him many things, including something quite serious: she had been the victim of sexual violence. Later on, A had the following dream:

> I am in a very strict school and they accuse me of rape, even if in the dream you cannot see the fact [. . .] the professors accuse me, but I haven't committed it, indeed it is the opposite, I was the one who got abused. They tell me that I will go to jail, they will do to me what I have done and I will die there. I say, "You are wrong, it didn't happen" and the dream ends when they are bringing me to jail [smiles and blushes a bit].

The patient's associations relate to a sense of "impotence" (in a text, a few days prior, he had written "I am helpless!").

The therapist commented that this feeling could relate to A's difficult circumstances of caring for his mother during her illness, for which he could not do anything. However, it could also relate to something else, tied to the past: the therapist referred to the feelings A had experienced during childhood, relating to his mother's abandonment, which left him feeling distressed and helpless.

Perhaps now that his mother was ill he felt guilty, because it was difficult for him to deal with the huge rage he had built over recent years, but never expressed. The patient responded to this interpretation with a long speech on the "positive sides" that his mother's gesture implied.

The therapist then made another comment on guilt:

> Perhaps, when you were little and your mother left, you felt that you were not doing enough for her, as if you didn't feel up to it and your love was not enough to stop her.

A replied:

> Yes, of course. . . partly it was like that.

The therapist commented that, indeed, even in the present he often did not feel up to it.

However, alongside this interpretation that connected A's aggression with his separation anxiety, the patient's fault also emerged from his sadistic defenses against the emotional bond, as manifested in a restless guilt towards the object that maniacally controlled and dominated him (through rape). The patient was anxious that the object (also in the transference) may be lost at any time. Rape was the sadistic attack that A feared to have led to his internal object.

The sadistic aspect of the ego identified with a split off aspect of the object—an aspect that could be thought of as an injunction full of hatred against a part of the self. This identification with the internal object that hated and was hated created a bond with an abusive object, on the side of either the victim or the perpetrator.

Session 43: 18 March 2014

This following session occurred one year into the psychotherapy treatment.

A spoke about his father, saying that there had never been dialogue between them. He had tried to establish one years prior, but ultimately gave up. Sitting on the sofa together allowed them to be close, but in a void—each surrounded by himself, without talking, with no exchange.

This experience of void and a lack of utility seems to have been made worse by eroding the desire to play. It was as if A was saying: "Now I really have nothing".

After looking down, as if he had had a sudden thought, A said: "I made note of three dreams". He read them by the phone:

> I am playing football [dream on Saturday night]. I play with Gabriele, a friend from secondary school; we play on a sidewalk and it is as if I saw myself from a window inside the school, we are in school hours [. . .] so I see myself through a glass.

A associated a carefree part of his life—his friendship with Gabriele—as something lighthearted and disinterested. He said in the dream that it felt melancholic to see himself in that way (as if something had been lost).

The glass may have evoked the presence of a psychic diaphragm— something standing between the self and the emotional experience, as if it were difficult for him to occupy the role of the child playing football. He could only look out the window, and could not participate, thus expressing detachment and an altered sense of self:

I am going to have a car accident [. . .] I didn't dream of the accident, but the moment is going to happen, fear, those feelings, as if I woke up the instant before the impact.

A said he missed the adrenaline of extreme things; this was something he no longer felt. The therapist commented that he must have tried to experience it by playing poker, and that this must have been a very powerful feeling. The dream, however, informs us of how risky it is to move on the wave of such violent emotions.

The third dream:

I am in a tournament, I arrived in a second position, but then I get beaten by an enemy of mine [tells me his name]. I am ashamed to have lost and I didn't say it at the moment, but only later.

Here, A's experience of defeat returns to his loss of skill—specifically, the expertise he felt he had in poker, his only skill. Maybe this is the source of his shame.

In general, A said that they seemed to have been three negative dreams. Having written down the dreams, despite the emptiness and catastrophic anxiety they reflected, in the company of an internal object with poor capacity to resist, seems to have been the first sign of a chance of a therapeutic bond, through the dream function.

The three dreams appear to have been a prelude to two absences in the following week. A melancholic feeling took shape—a painful and pervasive feeling that everything would gradually disappear. The adrenaline glitter of night playing and winning, the manic defenses and the omnipotence seem to have given way to a self-struggle with humiliating impotence. Humiliation generates shame and the need to hide from others' eyes. This psychic experience condemned A to stay in his bed and prevented him from attending sessions.

References

Bollas, C. (2008). *The Infinite Question*. London & New York: Routledge.
Freud, S. (1915b). Thoughts for the times on war and death. *S. E., 14*: 275–300. London: Hogarth.
Khan, M. (1963). The concept of cumulative trauma. *Psychoanalytic Study of the Child, 18*: 286–306.
Ogden, T. H. (2005). *This Art of Psychoanalysis: Dreaming Undreamt Dreams and Interrupted Cries*. London & New York: Routledge.
Winnicott, D. W. (1971). *Playing and Reality*. London & New York: Routledge.

CHAPTER SEVEN

Going through grief to move away from depression

Paolo Chiari

E very time I have started an analytic treatment with a patient showing clear symptoms of depression, I found myself dealing with doubts concerning the psychoanalytic theorisations about depression, starting from the writings of Abraham (1973[1912]) and Freud (1917e) up to the present. Indeed, it is difficult to establish whether the depressive process has to do with the object, its introjection in a part of the self, or the subject himself, with a collapse in self-esteem stemming from an imbalance between the Ideal of the self and how one's current self is perceived.

In this case, greater wellbeing, as Bibring (1953) and Sandler & Joffe (1965) claim, can be achieved by reappraising the ideal and adjusting it to the actual one, through some reorganisation: that is, a new individuation. Analytic work supports and develops the capacity to deal with psychic pain and the frustration caused by life situations. Depression can strike at any time in the life cycle, according to the studies mentioned in Northoff (2007), and psychodynamic imbalance also becomes a disorder of the systems that implies an involvement of concentric circles in both the subcortical and cortical areas of the brain.

However, if it is "the shadow of the object" falling on the subject that causes depression, psychoanalysis has the task of helping the patient to re-establish a new dialogue between the self and the object, by placing the latter outside the self, and to transform his superego that has become punitive and destructive (Freud, 1923b) and acting against the self, which is,, at the same time identified with the lost and ambivalently loved object.

In the clinical work, the two theories mentioned above can be brought together by focusing on the painful experience of separation–loss (in line with the studies carried out by Panksepp & Biven (2012) in recent decades). At an unconscious level, both the loss of the object and the loss of an idealised relationship generate a disappointing and threatening intrapsychic relation, in an entanglement of parts of the self and parts of the other. Moreover, we always need to keep in mind that depressive symptoms refer to a person with a personality structure (Gabbard, 1994; McWilliams, 1999). It is possible to see bipolar, masochistic, and narcissistic functioning quite early in the process of analysis. Finally as Freud emphasised (1917e), in melancholy one always finds guilt mixed with shame: we are in the complex area of the birth of the superego. (See Schore, 2008, for an important review of the literature about the appearance of shame.)

Clinical case: Fabio

For the first meeting, Fabio arrives almost thirty minutes later than the scheduled time. He immediately raises the issue of who is wrong, whose fault it is, the distance between my expectations and his. I just comment that, for sure, we are going to have only twenty minutes, but that time is all ours. His aggressiveness lessens and, after keeping silent for a while, he begins to cry quietly, lowering his head and hiding his face.

In the following sessions, I learn that Fabio is aged thirty-three, has a brother who is nineteen months younger, and he had lost his father unexpectedly. His father had been a self-made man who had worked hard, eventually becoming the manager of the technical department in a company. His father died in his arms when Fabio was sixteen, shortly after a quarrel with him, because the boy loved to go out and was not working hard enough at school. His mother, upset by her husband's death, was unable to help him. Soon, for practical reasons, he was forced to look for a job. A few years later, he married a good young woman, but he never established an emotionally and affectively meaningful relationship with her. Fabio recalls that after his father's death (he was electrocuted while fixing a household appliance), his life had completely changed. As I listen to him, I feel that, in spite of all the years that have gone by, the mourning process has not been completed yet.

After high school, Fabio tried to attend university for a few months, but was pervaded by a feeling of inadequacy. He had trouble making friends and was soon to drop out and give up his aspirations. The sense of lack of ability and failure when faced with this experience at university lasted for years. He fell back on odd jobs that increased the distance from his earlier dreams and expectations. In his life, a feeling of mortification and self-denigration prevailed, although his life improved when he was hired as a technician in a small company that was developing successfully. He felt his boss appreciated him and had the impression that he was himself again, realising his full potential. He put great commitment into his work, felt powerful, and dreamed about some professional success. Then the company was taken over by a multi-national corporation that introduced new criteria and working methods. A new position was created and a young graduate was appointed who became his boss. Fabio lost the direct and lively contact with his former boss that he was so fond of. He had to deal with the issue of not having a university degree, which was a requirement in the new working environment, and he started to experience his once-beloved company as a frustrating place. There, he felt helpless, humiliated, and a failure: shame crept in. His impression was that his path had reached its end and there was no exit.

At that point, he had a depressive breakdown. He felt depleted and full of anger against his boss, whom he regarded as having abandoned him; he lost interest in his job, had difficulty getting up in the morning, and was no longer excited about starting his working day. He was on sick leave for a few days, started to have digestive troubles, focused on his body, and became self-absorbed, until one day he was rude to his young boss. He received a warning letter from the company and, under pressure from his wife, a patient and reliable woman, he decided to ask for help.

I accepted him and suggested starting some work that could enable him to master his psychic pain better.

The beginning of the treatment is stormy. Fabio swings between angry criticism of his boss (in his transference against the analyst) and an over-estimation of his past role in the company, oscillating between idealising others and self-denigration, between his need for dependence and stating his own autonomy. He is susceptible to any intervention of mine and feels criticised and disparaged all the time. He often leaves the session feeling humiliated. He repeats that nothing can change; he says he is hopeless, but keeps on coming to analysis. What I offer is an emotionally constant understanding, some moments of emotional connection far from an intellectual level, because Fabio is self-focused, he ruminates about his mental states, recalls only the negative events, pays little attention to present experiences, and relies only on thinking. As I listen to him, I feel that an internalised, non-detached object is speaking. I wonder whether this has allowed Fabio to avoid anxiety and loneliness, and to maintain a sense of power against himself. His talk was often focused on the topics of power and social positions, so I prepare to deal with his narcissistic side, as well as his depressive symptomatology. That is why, as I keep in mind the studies on regulation and attunement of the relationship, I am co-operative every time misunderstandings or disruptions in communication occur.

I shall try to highlight his analytic process through some dreams he brought to therapy and fragments of dialogue from our sessions. Along this journey, which has lasted a few years, sessions concerning the mourning process for his father's death alternate with sessions where the patient describes his lack of ability and failures. As the therapy proceeds, feeling comforted and treated relieves his initial deep feeling of unhappiness and desolation. I quote a dream that shows the path he has covered in his mourning process.

P: I dreamt about my father. In the dream, he was in the bathroom and felt unwell. I helped him. I performed a cardiac massage and he slowly recovered. I told him he should not change the pipe of the washing machine by himself: "You cannot continue to do that all by yourself. You have to think about us as well."
[I realise that he has used the pronoun "us" for the first time.]
T: This time you managed to help and take care of him.
P: No, in fact my father had already passed away. I rushed and pulled him out but it wasn't enough.

T: In this dream, your father is once again available for a dialogue, an inner dialogue within yourself, and you talk to him again. Maybe, today, there could be the time that was missing yesterday.

P: Fifty minutes are too short to bring out all one's own pain.

T: I wonder if you are afraid that these walls and my mind are not able to hold that pain.

P: Yes.

T: You think that in any case nobody can give you back what you lost.

P: Yes. As long as the coffin was with us, he was there with us, but when the coffin was physically removed, there was a terrible pain. I began to cry. They told me not to. So, I stopped. [He bursts out crying.] How can I express the wish to go with him underground, to keep on staying with him forever? When he left . . . the air to breathe left as well. I wouldn't have changed the sheets, I would have kept his smell forever, I wouldn't have buried him far away, I wouldn't let the neighbouring places in the cemetery be taken.

Slowly, the work alliance becomes stronger. The topic of guilt leaves his talks. He starts to tell me about his actual life, his workplace, and his tasks. I listen to him carefully; I am interested in his reality, what he does. I accept his professional life in the session, I value his eight hours of effort that he devalues. He is surprised that his job—"this low-valued thing"—can have space in the consultation room, where he is confronted with an analyst who accepts his reality with interest.

At this point, Fabio offers a new dream that opens up a new chapter in his treatment.

I am with my wife in an abandoned, empty factory. It is Sunday. We find a place where we make love, we are good together, and we love each other. I turn to the side and I see our bodies in a mirror. They are beautiful. Suddenly, some people arrive and find us. I realise that the woman I made love with is not my wife any longer, but instead there is a man. I feel terribly ashamed and say, "It was nice, let's remember it like that."

He associates this dream with two episodes. The first one is about feeling handsome. He says, "Once, I went out for dinner with my wife and some of her colleagues. I liked myself. I felt particularly good. I had the impression that my wife showed me off to her co-workers. I went back home. I was alone, I looked in the mirror, and I felt attractive. I masturbated and I thought that in order to feel good I didn't need anyone".

The second episode with which he associates the dream concerns the sentence, "It was nice. Let's remember it like that." He remembers that he actually said that to a young woman and talks about a brief, never-confessed affair shortly after his engagement. They met three times in her apartment. Then, on their last date, he parted from her saying those words.

Fabio's dream and associations show me how important it is for him to be liked, to feel handsome, important, in a position of strength: acting rather than being subjugated, being appreciated, and feeling his grandiose self. These high demands prevent a balance between the natural need to be dependent, to have care and attention, and the drive to maintain his own autonomy. So, the further the analytic treatment proceeds, the more intense this struggle becomes. His dream introduces the difficult issue of shame. While it was relatively easy to accompany him in his mourning process, we are now confronted with a harder task. Shame does not refer so much to a conflict, but, rather, to the gap between the ego and the ego ideal, to omnipotent fantasies that cannot be fulfilled and, therefore, cannot access a welcoming inner space, are not accepted with warmth, and leave room for shame. Feeling handsome, being admired, and getting enjoyment all by himself through masturbation, and the role of the mirror, belong to an ideal, envied situation of wellbeing. But, in the same mirror, unexpected people appear and can observe that it is a homosexual (not ideal) relationship. It is the gaze of the other that generates shame. It seems to me that this dream expresses this functioning accurately.

In the following months, I observe how both old and new interests enter the scene and Fabio, at this point, can devote himself to them. Like a child, he tests himself in recently acquired skills and he experiments, somewhat exhilarated, with a variety of contexts. In a political group, he meets a woman of the same age, who has just separated (the ideal shifts outside); he feels drawn to her and starts a clandestine affair. Over time, he starts to meet her less and less, and the relationship ends when she falls in love with a man who is willing to build something together. In this whole period, I see his new interest in the outside world. Fabio starts to tell me more about his feelings; he reflects more thoroughly about his external reality, although he remains self-centred: it is the secret relationship with his lover, being desired and deciding when to meet the woman, that supports his self-esteem.

The end of the affair again causes a depressive response. Fabio is dealing with a separation that feels final and with the fact that what could be cannot be any more: his lover is not available; she refuses to meet him. He is aware he has not done anything to allow the relationship to develop further, but only now does he realise how supportive it was for him. The mirroring in the dream can be tackled at last.

P: You are saying that I am still trying to contact my lover who rejected me because sometimes I feel weak, painful, and I'm looking for some confirmation. Your words upset me. But now I'm not as angry as I used to be at the beginning of the treatment. This difference is possible because of the years we've spent together. Now it's easier for me to meet you without immediately feeling the need to seduce and surpass you. I have understood that the more the relationship feels asymmetrical, the stronger the pull is. It is triggered because I need to seduce someone who feels powerful to me. I was reminded of the dream where I was making love, looked in the mirror, and saw myself handsome, but then found myself with a man and people were looking at me. I remember that I associated that dream with an event that embarrassed me very much—masturbating in front of the mirror—yet I told you about it. So, I thought that both the relationship with my lover and the relationship with you have to do with the mirror. Mirroring exhilarates me. In the rendezvous with my lover, we were mutually mirroring, masturbating at length without really feeling that we reached one another. There was no real meeting, although the affair did have some exciting moments. If mirroring was what one sought, that relationship was wonderful. But it wasn't a real relationship. The real relationship is not a mirror that shows you only what you like; you don't like everything of the other. My wife is real. A real relationship is different from one where you take only what you need.

T: If I understand correctly, you are saying that there are masturbatory relationships and full relationships. One can use the other or meet the other.

P: I think so. I've started making love with my wife again. I feel good, but there isn't the erotic play there was with my lover. In an affair, you take what you want; it isn't a cynical exploitation, but you can take just what you need. She talked about her loneliness, but I couldn't take those aspects in.

T: With your lover, you felt accepted and desired for a long time, the two of you as one thing in your hands, but then you felt rejected.

P: The mirror shattered, but I keep on trying to mirror myself in the pieces, in the fragments of mirror that are left. What these pieces reflect is an unsatisfactory image, but now I can bear it. There isn't just disappointment. I know I leaned on my lover and on this therapy because I was looking for some mirroring that could ensure a constant balance to confirm me as a strong and successful man.

We had to go through more treatment before a new dream appeared. It introduced the possibility of changes that would not damage or upset.

P: Last night I fell asleep, thinking that today I would come to you to tell you everything that happened over the weekend, and I had a dream. I dreamt I came here. But instead of you, I found a woman and some other people. I wondered why I should talk to the woman, or to the other people, but then I calmed down and thought I could. If they were here, I could trust them, and you would arrive later.

T: It seems that there is room for some changes that don't have the feature of lasting forever. We can meet again and reunite. There's also room for a woman and other people. One can be replaced, but not for ever. Only death forces us to that.

P: That's exactly it. As far as changes are concerned, I wanted to tell you that I was reminded we had to move house when I was at junior high school. Because of that I had to part from my first love. It was very painful; leaving meant great sorrow. It meant I had to make space for something I didn't desire. Now I know that, aside from death, the worst moments are like a sea storm; the sea can cover the coastline but then the land re-emerges, comes back, and this ceaseless back and forth of the waves goes on as long as life exists, with its inevitable finality.

I like to think that, in the woman who has replaced me in the dream, in the possibility of finding me again, in bidding his adolescent love farewell, there is farewell and reunion with his first real love, that is, his mother.

Eighteen months later, Fabio, who was then in his forties, felt that separation from analysis was going to be possible. I agreed with this decision, because he seemed to have an emotional model that enabled him not to necessarily repeat his past experiences: a mature disillusion had replaced his impossible illusion of being stronger and winning over the others. Now, he was able not to experience every relationship as a competing one and to tolerate the pain that life imposes through inevitable separations, whether they are internal or external.

From the account of this clinical case, one can assume a path, dream after dream, that allowed the patient to go through grief and move away from depression to finally come to a good, integrated, psychosomatic–neurovegetative functioning:

- in the first dream, where he resuscitates his father, although the denial and manic reparation (nothing happened) are evident, the patient can finally share his huge pain;
- in the second dream, where he associates his feeling admired by his wife's girlfriends with masturbation, one can clearly see the supportive role of an external object;
- in the same dream, the patient is seen while he makes love with a man. There is mirroring and narcissistic withdrawal (I do not need the lost object) but also the difficult experience of shame he feels in being discovered in a situation that is socially unacceptable;
- in the third dream (with the woman analyst) the possibility of a new object replacing the former one appears;
- eventually, normal physiology seems to have returned: the land can re-emerge after the battering of the heavy sea: his contact with the psychosomatic–neurovegetative functioning marks the resumption of the breath of life in the flow of the waves.

References

Abraham, K. (1973)[1912]. Notes on the psychoanalytic investigation and treatment of manic-depressive insanity and allied conditions. In: *Selected Papers on Psycho-Analysis* (pp. 137–156). London: Hogarth.

Bibring, E. (1953). The mechanism of depression. In P. Greenacre (Ed.), *Affective Disorders: Psychoanalytic Contributions to Their Study* (pp. 13–48). Oxford, UK: International Universities Press.

Freud, S. (1917e). Mourning and melancholia. *S. E.*, 14: 239–258. London: Hogarth.

Freud, S. (1923b). *The Ego and the Id. S. E., 19*: 3–66. London: Hogarth.

Gabbard, G. (1994). *Psychodynamic Psychiatry in Clinical Practice.* Arlington VA: American Psychiatric Publishing.

McWilliams, N. (1999). *Psychoanalytic Diagnosis.* New York: Guilford Press.

Northoff, G. (2007). Psychopathology and pathophysiology of the self in depression: neuropsychiatric hypothesis. *Journal of Affective Disorders, 104*(1–3): 1–14.

Panksepp, J., & Biven, L. (2012). *The Archaeology of Mind.* New York: W. W. Norton.

Sandler, J., & Joffe, W. G. (1965). Notes on childhood depression. *International Journal of Psychoanalysis, 46*: 88–96.

Schore, A. (2008). *Affect Regulation and the Repair of the Self.* New York: W. W. Norton.

CHAPTER EIGHT

What can neuroscience contribute to the interpretation of dreams and their working through? A clinical case

Francesco Castellet y Ballarà

Introduction

Marcia is a young, single, adult woman who is financially independent. She is in analysis, three sessions a week, and uses the couch. Partly as the result of the analytic work, she left her parents' home and lives alone. Nevertheless, she is very involved in her parents' severely conflictual relationship, and her mother often ambivalently requires her support.

Marcia has one sister, some years younger than her, who is her closest ally in the continuously tense family atmosphere.

She (Marcia) is struggling with her emotional life as lesbian, and seems to be unable to maintain a stable and satisfying relationship with a partner.

She fears she might be and behave like her father, in the sense of becoming violent and suspiciously jealous if the relation is not close and constant enough. At the same time, she tends to feel constrained and suffocated when there is too much closeness. This was the main reason why she came into treatment.

When Marcia was still an adolescent, her mother moved for a couple of years to another town for working reasons. During that time,

Marcia had to deal with the emotional instability of her father, whose care rested mostly on her shoulders.

She brought two dreams featuring screams. This is the first one:

> My sister was tied up in a dentist chair and my father and my mother were cutting her face with a razor. I was full of rage and yelled at them "assholes, assholes". Then I thought that I had to accustom myself to addressing them like that.

On further enquiry about her emotions during the dream, she focuses on her rage towards the mother, who is usually considered to be just the victim of the violent father. Then, suddenly, she links the dream to her mother's invitation to join the family for the sister's birthday. It looked like a trap: she will again become involved in fights with her father.

The second dream:

> I was at home and it was dark. I was scared by the presence of a crazy priest whose robe was decorated with pictures of angels and demons.

When asked by the analyst to associate more on the fear of craziness, the patient says:

> I fear darkness, still. Probably because the nights at home, during childhood, were a complete nightmare due to my parents' furious fights. On such nights, I heard words such as "have mercy" or "then, kill me" but next morning, everybody acted as if nothing happened, even though there was some broken stuff around. My mother never touched on, or opened up, this issue with anyone. I felt confused and doubtful about my recollections of the events. Was I the one crazy, or was she? Or both, my dad and my mum? Surely, angels and demons remind me of the hell I lived in at home. Often, when I wake up after some nightmarish sleep, I suffer from a kind of hallucination: the ceiling seems to move downwards as if to smash me, or as if it is under the control of aliens that torture me. At other times, a swarm of bees threatens me by flying around the room.

Discussion

Dreaming, defined by Freud (1900a) as "The royal road to the unconscious", is still a critical tool in the exploration of our patients' emotional life and a specificity of analytic technique. The recent advances in neuroscience and infant research (Fischmann et al., 2013; Panksepp & Biven, 2012; Solms, 1995) could provide additional empirical support to psychoanalytic theories of dreaming, since they underline the centrality of emotions in determining and understanding human dream narratives. In fact, in the clinical case briefly outlined above, the emotional content of both dreams is characterised by terror provoked by scary and torturing parental figures—instead of reassuring ones—and by the intense rag felt towards them.

In addition, the fear of darkness, the startle responses at the slightest unexpected sound, the hallucination-like persecutory phenomena at the moment of awakening, fit well with the traumatic nature of her probably dysregulating attachment (Hill, 2015) with the parents, so clearly depicted in her nightmares and dreams.

According to the latest neuroscientific contribution (Blundo, 2011), we can, paradoxically, define dreaming as "a state of consciousness" occurring not only during REM sleep, but also during NREM sleep, even if the characteristics are different: NREM dreams are less vivid and less emotionally rich compared to the REM dreams.

Dreaming is the final product of the activation of complex neural networks in several cognitive domains responsible for attention, memory, language in general, and sensorial perception and visual imagery (Braun et al., 1997; Nofzinger et al., 1997; Solms, 1997). These networks are active during sleep while dreaming as well as during awakening (Schwartz & Maquet, 2002), supporting Bion's proposal of considering daydreaming a physiological aspect of awakening mental life (Bion, 1991).

Therefore, most probably, dreaming cannot be the result of a random collection of emotions, perceptions, or memories, as in a confusional state of consciousness (delirium), but it has an internal structure of its own that mirrors the ongoing cognitive and emotional processes especially: in my opinion, the more emotionally and motivationally relevant (Schwartz & Maquet, 2002).

Marcia's marked difficulties in intimate relations can be better understood as the result of chronic invasion of the content of her nightmares in her daily relational life. This invasion, or interference with her reality testing, does not attain the severity of a psychotic state (frank hallucinations and delusions), but it is sufficiently pervasive to distort her reading of the other's behaviours and wording in difficult relational situations. Actually, she cannot rely on her first impressions of the other's behaviour since they are, under stress, regularly deformed in a persecutory way, dominated by the other's unreliability as a loving person and her own belief in her unworthiness.

This borderline type of thinking can be correlated with some recent findings in attachment disorders studies and the neurobiology of traumatic memories (Schore, 2012).

Neuroimaging techniques, during dreaming, show how the prototypical sensorimotor hallucinations, the hyper-emotionality, and the cognitive distortions are correlated with patterns of activations/deactivations of specific brain regions (Solms, 1997).

It is of particular interest to the analyst that activation of limbic and paralimbic structures (in particular, the amygdala) during REM sleep has been observed (Solms, 1995).

This could explain the very common negative emotional (fear and anxiety) content of many dreams, because the amygdala is known to be the structure where negative emotions such as fear are stored (Nader et al., 2000).

It would seem, therefore, that consolidation of long term memory, both implicit and explicit, is a sleep–dreaming dependent process (Sejnowski & Destexhe, 2000; Stickgold, 1998).

The affects of traumatic memories are then stored in the amygdala and are elicited by context dependent perceptions that, particularly under stress, might disturb a correct reading of events in the reality (Nader et al., 2000).

Motivation is also an important aspect of the dream genesis. Solms (2000) proved that neurological patients suffering from deep frontal ventromedial lesions (the centre of motivation in the prefrontal cortex) had a complete absence of dreaming.

So, motivation and emotions (ventral prefrontal cortex and amygdala) are crucial to dream formation and, therefore, as analysts, we should pay focused attention to these elements of dreams in order to formulate a transformative interpretation in our clinical setting, possibly helping to consolidate an alternative emotional memory of the traumatic event as a consequence of the therapeutic relation.

Trauma-related disorders can be characterised by a specific kind of memory, made of somatic traces, difficult to be transformed into words (Van der Kolk, 2014), but easily influencing dream formation, in particular their emotional content.

The iconic language of dreams seems to be resistant, or resilient, to massive psychic trauma that is, verbally, by definition, "mute" (Volkan, 2014), but not blind. In the case of PTSD, trauma-related nightmares and terrifying daydreams/hallucinations flood the victim's mind in a desperate attempt to find another mind to provide meaning and relief through an alternative experience of emotional matching.

We know (Alberini, 2011) that the phenomenon of false memories affects the dream's context, its sensorial data, time frame, or places that could be mixed up or distorted, but not the dream emotions, which are usually well preserved and, hence, could serve as a reliable guide to understanding the dream.

Moreover, dreams are always emotion-ridden and only defence mechanisms during waking can deprive them of these crucial elements. At the same time, dream amnesia is so common that it seems obvious to think of dreaming as a secret endeavour that needs to be taken separately from consciousness most of the time in order to function properly.

Could it be that awareness of some relational emotional realities is too traumatic to be sustained without an empathic listener?

This is true especially in the first stages of life when the immaturity of the brain structures forces the newborn to rely totally and dramatically on the carer for self-regulation of his physiological and emotional states, that is, for survival (Tronick, 2003).

Infantile amnesia is a well-known phenomenon (the usual lack of memory of the events before three to four years of age) and seems to be related to the immaturity of the memory systems (hippocampus) and the impossibility of consolidating long-term memories (Travaglia et al., 2016), but, maybe, memories are preserved in other ways, unconscious and implicit, within the mind–body.

From the research on attachment, for example, we have data (see Coan, 2008) on the locus coeruleus of the newborn as the structure responsible for the consolidation of the memories of the carers' faces, voices, and smells in a temporal stage when the amygdala is not yet properly functioning.

Therefore, at this stage, an aversive conditioning is difficult or impossible, and then almost all the inputs are classified simply as familiar or safe, irrespective of their effects. Maltreatments could then be assimilated as "good or normal" and attachment made possible and, later in life, replicated as biases for internal working models in interpersonal relations (Coan, 2008).

Marcia's case, with her frequent and terrifying nightmares concerning relational traumatic failures as well as the repetition compulsion to replicate these same failures in every new relationship, could be a clear example of how dreams express, in iconic and emotional language, the early relational traumata that shaped her body–mind.

References

Alberini, C. M. (2011). The role of reconsolidation and the dynamic process of long-term memory formation and storage. *Frontiers in Behavioral Neuroscience*, 5: 12.

Bion, W. R. (1991). *Cogitations*. London: Karnac.

Blundo, C. (2011). *Neuroscienze cliniche del comportamento*. Milan: Elsevier.

Braun, A. R., Balkin, T. J., Wesenten, N. J., Carson, R. E., Varga, M., Baldwin, P., Selbie, S., Belenky, G., & Herscovitch, P. (1997). Regional blood flow throughout the sleep–wake cycle. *Brain*, 120: 1173–1197.

Coan, J. A. (2008). Towards a neuroscience of attachment. In: J. Cassidy & P. R. Shaver (Eds.), *Handbook of Attachment: Theory, Research, and Clinical Application* (3rd edn) (pp. 241–265). New York: Guilford Press.

Fischmann, T., Russ, M. O., & Leuzinger-Bohleber, M. (2013). Trauma, dream, and psychic change in psychoanalyses: a dialog between psychoanalysis and the neurosciences. *Frontiers in Human Neuroscience*, 7(877): 1–15. doi: 10.3389/fnhum.2013.00877.

Freud, S. (1900a). *The Interpretation of Dreams. S. E.*, 4–5. London: Hogarth.

Hill, D. (2015). *Affect Regulation Theory: A Clinical Model*. New York: W. W. Norton.

Nader, K., Schafe, G. E., & LeDoux, J. E. (2000). Fear memories require protein synthesis in the amygdala for reconsolidation after retrieval. *Nature*, 406: 722–726.

Nofzinger, E., Mintun, M., Wiseman, M., Kupfer, D., & Moore, R. (1997). Forebrain activation in REM sleep: an FDG PET study. *Brain Research*, 770: 169–201.

Panksepp, J., & Biven, L. (2012). *The Archeology of the Mind: Neuroevolutionary Origins of Human Emotions*. New York: W. W. Norton.

Schore, A. (2012). *The Science of the Art of Psychotherapy*. New York: W. W. Norton.

Schwartz, S., & Maquet, P. (2002). Sleep imaging and the neuropsychological assessment of dreams. *Trend Cognitive Science, 6*(1): 23–30.

Sejnowski, T., & Destexhe, A. (2000). Why do we sleep? *Brain Research, 886*: 208–233.

Solms, M. (1995). New findings on the neurological organization of dreaming: implications for psychoanalysis. *Psychoanalytic Quarterly, 64*: 43–67.

Solms, M. (1997). *The Neuropsychology of Dreams.* Mahwah, NJ: Lawrence Erlbaum.

Solms, M. (2000). Dreaming and REM sleep are controlled by different brain mechanisms. *Behavioral and Brain Sciences, 23*: 843–850.

Stickgold, R. (1998). Sleep: off-line memory processing. *Trends in Cognitive Sciences, 2*: 484–492.

Travaglia, A., Bisaz, R., Sweet, E. S., Blitzer, R. D., & Alberini, C. M. (2016). Infantile amnesia reflects a developmental critical period for hippocampal learning. *Nature Neuroscience, 19*: 1225–1233.

Tronick, E. Z. (2003). Of course, all relationships are unique. *Psychoanalytic Inquiry, 23*(3): 473–491.

Van der Kolk, B. (2014). *The Body Keeps the Score.* New York: Penguin.

Volkan, V. D. (2014). *Animal Killer: Transmission of War Trauma from One Generation to the Next.* London: Karnac.

CHAPTER NINE

Conclusions: bridging the gap

Claudia Spadazzi

I t is not by chance that the need for a dialogue between psycho-analysis and neuroscience was felt for the first time in the late 1900s, at the end of the century characterised by the birth, the success, and also the crisis, of psychoanalysis. It is difficult to think of a development of psychoanalysis in the following century, in the new millennium, without building not one, but many bridges between the opposite sides of the two disciplines, neuroscience and psychoanalysis.

Thinking back to the dawn of this dialogue, it is impossible not to recall the exciting atmosphere of the 44th IPA Congress in New Orleans, when Antonio Damasio, in his *lectio magistralis*, projected some neuroimaging videos (the first ever seen by most psychoanalysts in the room) on neuronal functions and emphasised their unconscious aspects. Distinguished senior colleagues were sitting in the first rows of the packed conference room. Damasio approached Daniel Wid-locher, at that time President of the IPA, on the podium and jokingly stressed how "close" he felt to psychoanalysis. The audience laughed out loud at this joke; no one knows the extent to which they were aware that they were perhaps witnessing the laying of the first "stone" of the "bridge". Therefore, Damasio's lecture at the 2004 IPA Congress served to make official a dialogue that had been started a decade earlier by Damasio (1994), Kandel (1999), LeDoux (1996), Panksepp (1998), Solms (2004) and was formalised by the space and the recognition given by the IPA to this highly distinguished and already extremely famous neuroscientist.

Building a bridge takes a long time and a lot of work: design, works supervision, high costs, work progress, checks, testing. At present, the plan of the "bridge" is still sketchy. For the time being, some pioneers are providing tentative contributions to the foundations of what will finally be an executive plan. The "works supervision" spontaneously ended up within the framework of Mark Solms's work, Chair of the IPA Research Commission (2013–2017). In his double roles as neuroscientist and psychoanalyst, he has always worked to pave a way to dialogue and compatibility between the two disciplines. Most distinguished colleagues who are contributing to building the "bridge" have been trained in both domains: among others, Yoram Yovell, Maggie Zellner, Cristina Alberini, Katerina Fotopoulou, and Oliver Turnbull.

The etymology of the word "bridge" in neo-Latin languages (Lat: *pons*, Greek: *pònto*, Sanskrit *matrix: path*) refers to "going", to "connecting", and to "moving back and forth". Sometimes, bridges were used for invasions and conquests; in fact, during the empire, the Romans were master builders of bridges. Some of them are still used after two millennia: for example, Ponte Milvio across the Tiber river in Rome. Historically, bridges were equated with progress, since they paved the way to dialogue and trade, to the promotion of cultural cross-fertilisation and to easier transactions.

Psychoanalysis is well known to have difficulty in talking to related sciences, in particular with psychiatry and other medical domains, for a series of reasons that date back to the very origins of this discipline. The distance from university departments, the impossibility of using a common language with other sciences, the poor systemisation of data, the tendency of analysts to work alone, a certain disregard of the opinion of the scientific community, have pushed psychoanalysis to become increasingly isolated, in a different way according to its geographical location and to its social milieu, and to become self-referential (Kernberg, 2012); in turn, this has led psychoanalysis to be considered as a "science of its own".

Even Stefano Bolognini (President of the IPA 2013–2017) declared (with Simona Argentieri, Luigi Zoja, and Antonio Di Ciaccia), in a sort of "manifesto" published on 22 February 2012, in the Italian newspaper *La Repubblica*, that psychoanalysis is "a science with a special autonomy" which "explores the unconscious (its specific historical and substantial field) as well as the relations between conscious and unconscious, the deep interrelations existing at various levels within an individual and various individuals within a couple, a group, a community." This might be so. However, in considering it a "science of its own", one could be tempted to exempt it from exchanging with other sciences and overlook the fertile interaction with its most similar sciences, such as psychiatry and the neurosciences. The speed of scientific progress is something which today's generation of psychoanalysts must face.

The matters of mind *vs.* body and monism *vs.* dualism (Churchland, 2013; Damasio, 1994; Erreich, 2016; Nagel, 1974; Panksepp, 2005) have been for centuries the hinge of well-articulated dialectics between philosophers, theologians, and scientists. Over the past twenty years, the intrusion of recent acquisitions proposed by neurosciences— offering an astronomical amount of both experimental and theoretical data—has made dialoguing unavoidable. The data cannot be interpreted unambiguously; it is sometimes contradictory, at other times illuminating or deceiving. Psychoanalysts and psychotherapists, initially perplexed, have taken different stands towards this discipline that has, for the past ten years, offered complex and significant contributions by using sophisticated technologies, clinical data, and psychodynamic tests and experiments. By far more comprehensible to the scientific community, neurosciences risk overlapping with psychoanalysis in that they both deal with the same compelling and elusive material. The general attitude of psychoanalysts and psychotherapists wavers between curiosity and denial, with a wide range of intermediate positions. At one extreme, we can find interest and open-mindedness; at the other extreme, there are others entrenched in a preconceived refusal. Some extremist attitudes are so strongly felt as to condemn one's simple interest or curiosity as deceptive, if not even Messianic.

André Green's position is very clear: "One must admit that a quotation from Shakespeare can be more illuminating, for a psychoanalyst, than a ton of scientific literature" (2001). However, psychoanalytic literature declaring an open opposition to neuroscience is rather limited (Edelson, 1986; Smith, 1997). Even in his well-known article bearing the provocative title "On the astonishing clinical irrelevance of neuroscience" (2003), Pulver explains that he is only alluding to the irrelevance to the psychoanalytic method, not to the general clinical work, and his conciliatory conclusion is that "Neuroscience and psychoanalysis need each other". The issue of relevance is also pointed out by Canestri (2015), who concludes supporting dialogue because neurosciences deepens the undestanding of psychic phenomena and provides tools for therapeutic intervention.

Since 2007, the controversy between the two factions has been well represented by distinguished colleagues (Yovell et al., 2015 *vs*. Blass & Carmeli, 2007, 2015, 2016) who have braved one another in an intense discussion mostly over theoretic matters, although they have sometimes referred to clinical data. Among others, the controversy has been commented by Kessler (2016) and Sandberg (2016) in the *International Journal of Psychoanalysis*, followed by Blass and Carmeli's response. In attempting to summarise, in general terms, the main points the two fields have been battling over, one can look at the basic controversy outlined by Blass and Carmeli as bearing on:

1. The relevance of neurosciences with regard to theoretical and clinical psychoanalysis;
2. The non-analytic nature of neurosciences'
3. The potentially harmful effects of neurosciences on psychoanalysis.

Let us us look, for example, at an Original Research Article, "Assessment of emotional experience and emotional recognition in complicated grief" published in 2016 by Turnbull and other authors in *Frontiers in Psychology* (Fernández-Alcántara et al., 2016).

The article illustrates some recent experimental data on complicated grief (CG)—the prolonged grief following bereavement. According to this research, patients who develop CG are incapable of facing the loss and more generally have serious difficulty with emotional adjustment. Six or twelve months after the loss, these patients are still suffering a great deal, showing feelings of guilt, anger, sadness; they are incapable of accepting the loss, feel lost, and lose sight of the meaning of life (Prigerson et al., 2008). These patients often have difficulty in adjusting emotionally and in expressing their emotions. In underlining the difference between the perception and expressing of emotions and the subjective experience of emotions (Adolphs & Damasio, 2000;

Damasio et al., 2000; Panksepp, 1998; Panksepp & Watt, 2011), the authors suggest that patients with complicated grief implement the dopaminergic SEEKING system, similarly to addicted patients. In fact, according to the authors, the functioning of various subcortical structures involved in the processing of emotions is altered. In particular, the nucleus accumbens, as well as the amygdala and the orbitofrontal cortex, appear to be hyperactive. The differential diagnosis between bereavement and depression was already underlined by Freud in "Mourning and melancholia" in 1917, when he outlines that the painful job of mourning is the withdrawal of libido from the lost object and "when the work is completed, the ego becomes free and uninhibited again" (Freud, 1917e, pp. 244–245). Conversely, in cases of depression, the libido invested in the lost object is brought back to the ego and the ego identifies with the lost one. "The object-loss was transformed into an ego-loss", argued Freud, "and the conflict between the ego and the loved person into a cleavage between the critical activity of the ego and the ego as altered by identification" (p. 249).

V. D. Volkan (1984) clarifies the difference between mourning and pathological mourning from a psychoanalytic perspective, and suggests to consider different approaches in relation to other psycho-pathologic aspects of the patient's personality. H. Bleichmar (2010) proposes a psychoanalytical nosology of pathological mourning: fixation to the lost object due to narcissistic anxieties; secondary idealisation—after loss—as a condition fixating to the lost object; fixation to the lost object because of persecutory anxieties, which is a helpful tool to obtain indications for a differentiated treatment, in order to recognise which will be able to modify and which will reinforce pathology. Now, in 2017, exactly 100 years after Freud's "Mourning and melancholia", we are able try to link the "shadow of the object" to the activity of neurotransmitters. In cases of depression, the PANIC/GRIEF system is hyperactive whereas the activity of the SEEKING system appears to be reduced. In terms of libido, it would appear that in mourning, and especially pathological mourning, the ego does not resign itself to the loss, persists in seeking, and denies reality. The balance between the SEEKING and PANIC/GRIEF systems is equivalent to psychodynamic adjustments between the ego, the lost object. and reality. Depression entails a sort of resignation, as if seeking itself loses meaning. Solms and Panksepp (2010) argue that the core brain basis for depression revolves around the process by which separation distress is normally shut down (possibly by kappa-opioids), prompting the animal to "give up".

In Chapter Three, in this book, Mark Solms describes extensively the mechanisms of depression from a neuropsychoanalytic perspective, with the aim to overcome the gap between a psychopharmacological understanding and the psychotherapeutic understanding. He argues that "the core brain basis for depression revolves around the process by which separation distress is normally shut down (possibly by kappa-opioids like dynorphin), prompting the animal to 'give up'". To be able to understand the difference between depression and complicated grief, not only from a clinical or theoretical point of view, but also from a psychopharmacological point of view, can be a useful tool to orient the treatment.

Regarding Blass and Carmeli' s position, it seems difficult to understand how the information in Turnbull's article could be considered (a) irrelevant and even (c) harmful. With regard to (b) "non-analytical", the matter is significant and fundamental. But how can one establish what is analytical and what is not? Does it not depend upon how a concept, the data, and the relations are used? In a present that no longer distinguishes between scientific culture and humanistic culture, does a psychoanalyst's culture not enhance one's capacity to enter into contact with the Other?

Deciding to not avail oneself of fact-finding means related to an area so close to one's own could border on obscurantism. On the other hand, the history of science reminds us of many pioneers who were opposed by the scientific establishments of their time, with disastrous consequences for the scholars themselves and the community, Ignaz Semmelweiss and his personal and tragic fight against puerperal fever being just one example.[1]

One could theorise that the psychoanalytic community is, presently, both psychologically and collectively, in a condition wavering between depression and complicated grief. The age of dogmatic, elitist, self-referential psychonalysis has come and gone. In 1910, during the second International Congress of Psychoanalysis in Nuremberg, Freud declared that the future of psychoanalysis depended on three factors: "internal progress, greater prestige and the general effects of our work". He concluded his speech specifying that psychoanalysts should "work in the service of science", "giving to patients the most efficacious remedy for their suffering available at the present time"

(1910d, pp. 141–142). With new ways of understanding psychological suffering being brought to light by recent acquisitions in neurosciences, are we not compelled to an update and debate between these and the theoretical corpus of psychoanalysis? Would not an *a priori* avoidance run the risk of impeding a development and fossilising psychoanalysis into a "dinosaur", to which Peter Medawar (Nobel Prize winner in 1960 with MacFarlane Burnet for immune tolerance mechanisms) said,

> Considered in its entirety, psychoanalysis won't do. It is an end product, moreover, like a dinosaur or a zeppelin, no better theory can ever be erected on its ruins, which will remain forever one of the saddest and strangest of landmarks in the history of twentieth century thought. (p. 130)

What future could there be for a psychoanalytic community that wishes not to include neurosciences in its training and fears change? What defence mechanisms are being put in place to prevent the possibility of change—one of the aims of a psychoanalytic therapy? Could it be because it frightens and puts in check the psychoanalysts who advocate and promote this possibility and the importance of change?

Robert Michels (2010) expresses his concern about the length of a transoceanic "bridge". Michels argues how the neuroscientific developments are fundamentally related with obsolete psychoanalytic concepts, mainly metapsychological, and not with transference–countertransference dynamics, with intersubjective aspects, and with the concept of co-construction. However, integration needs time and, for a future effective synergic co-operation between the two disciplines, a new generation is necessary: neuroscientists interested to the inner world and young psychoanalysts skilled in the brain's biologic functioning. Within the next decade, the study of neurosciences—regarding the basic functioning of neural networks and neurotransmitters, the neuroendocrine and neuroimmunological implications, the acquisitions in gene expression of memory, the theories on the development of the consciousness, the neurological basis of affects, the experimental data on dream functioning—will, one hopes, be integrated within the curriculum of training analysts. The Psychoanalytic Societies and the IPA have the responsibility to avoid letting too much water flow under the bridge.

Note

1. Ignaz Semmelweiss (1818–1865), pioneer in the fight against puerperal fever, lived and worked in Vienna where he was opposed and eventually expelled from the university. He died in a psychiatric hospital in tragic circumstances. His fundamental scientific contribution was only acknowledged after his death. "La vie et l'oeuvre de Philippe Ignace Semmelweiss" was the writer Céline's dissertation in medicine.

References

Adolphs, R., & Damasio, A. R. (2000). Neurobiology of emotion at a systems level. In: J. C. Borod (Ed.), *The Neuropsychology of Emotion* (194–213). New York: Oxford University Press.

Blass, R. B., & Carmeli, Z. (2007). The case against neuropsychoanalysis. *International Journal of Psychoanalysis, 88*: 19–40.

Blass, R. B., & Carmeli, Z. (2015). Further evidence for the case against neuropsychoanalysis: how Yovell, Solms and Fotopoulou's response to our critique confirms the irrelevance and harmfulness to psychoanalysis of the contemporary neuroscientific trend. *International Journal of Psychoanalysis, 96*: 1555–1573.

Blass, R. B., & Carmeli, Z. (2016). Response to Kessler, Sandberg, and Busch: the case for and against neuropsychoanalysis. *International Journal of Psychoanalysis, 97*: 1155–1158.

Bleichmar, H. (2010). Rethinking pathological mourning: multiple types and therapeutic approaches. *Psychoanalytic Quarterly, 79*: 71–93.

Canestri, J. (2015). The case for neuropsychoanalysis. *International Journal of Psychoanalysis, 96*: 1575–1584.

Churchland, P. S. (2013). *Touching a Nerve. The Self as Brain*. New York: W. W. Norton.

Damasio, A. R. (1994). *Descartes' Error: Emotion, Reason and the Human Brain*. New York: Grosset/Putnam.

Damasio, A. R., Grabowski, T. J., Bechara, A., Damasio, H., Ponto, L. L., Parvizi, J., & Hichwa, R. D. (2000). Subcortical and cortical brain activity during the feeling of self-generated emotions. *Nature Neuroscience, 3*: 1049–1056.

Edelson, M. (1986). The convergence of psychoanalysis and neuroscience: illusion and reality, *Contemporary Psychoanalysis, 22*: 479–519.

Erreich, A. (2016). An exchange with Thomas Nagel. The mind–body problem and psychoanalysis. *Journal of the American Psychoanalytical Association, 64*: 389–403.

Fernández-Alcántara, M., Cruz-Quintana, F., Pérez-Marfil, M. N., Catena-Martínez, A., Pérez-García, M., & Turnbull, O. H. (2016). Assessment of emotional experience and emotional recognition in complicated grief. *Frontiers in Psychology, 7*: 126.

Freud, S. (1910d). The future prospects of psychoanalytic therapy. *S. E., 11*: 139–158. London: Hogarth.

Freud, S. (1917e). Mourning and melancholia. *S. E., 14*: 239–254. London: Hogarth.

Green, A. (2001). Advice to psychoanalysts: 'Cognitive psychology is good for you'. Commentary on Semenza's paper—Psychoanalysis and cognitive neuropsychology: theoretical and methodological affinities. *Neuropsychoanalysis, 3*(1): 16–19.

Kandel, E. R. (1999). Biology and the future of psychoanalysis: a new intellectual framework for psychiatry revisited. *American Journal of Psychiatry, 156*: 505–524.

Kernberg, O. F. (2012). Suicide prevention for psychoanalytic institutes and societies. *Journal of the American Psychoanalytic Association, 60*(4): 707–719.

Kessler, L. (2016). Commentary on 'The case for neuropsychoanalysis'. *International Journal of Psychoanalysis, 97*: 1145–1147.

LeDoux, J. E. (1996). *The Emotional Brain.* New York: Simon and Schuster.

Medawar, P. B. (1996). *The Strange Case of the Spotted Mice and Other Classic Essays on Science.* New York: Oxford University Press.

Michels, R. (2010). Psychoanalysis and neuroscience: ten years later. A roundtable discussion. Available at: www.youtube.com/watch?v=zlkliGaIBQI.

Nagel, T. (1974). What is it like to be a bat?. *The Philosophical Review, 83*(4): 435–450.

Panksepp, J. (1998). *Affective Neuroscience. The Foundation of Human and Animal Emotion.* New York: Oxford University Press.

Panksepp, J. (2005). Affective consciousness: core emotional feelings in animals and humans. *Consciousness and Cognition, 14*(1): 30–80.

Panksepp, J., & Watt, D. (2011). What is basic about basic emotions? Lasting lessons from affective neuroscience. *Emotion Review, 3*: 387–396.

Prigerson, H. G., Vanderwerker, L. C., & Maciejewski, P. K. (2008). Prolonged grief disorder: a case for inclusion in DSM-V. In: M. S.

Stroebe (Ed.), *Handbook of Bereavement Research and Practice: Advances in Theory and Intervention* (pp. 165–186). Washington, DC: American Psychological Association.

Pulver, S. E. (2003). On the astonishing clinical irrelevance of neuroscience. *Journal of the American Psychoanalytic Association, 51*(3): 755–772.

Sandberg, L. S. (2016). On the argument for (and against) neuropsychoanalysis. *International Journal of Psychoanalysis, 97*: 1149–1150.

Smith, H. F. (1997). Creative misreading: why we talk past each other. *Journal of the American Psychoanalytic Association, 45*: 335–357.

Solms, M. (2004). Freud returns. *Scientific American, 290*: 82–88.

Solms, M., & Panksepp, J. (2010). Why depression feels bad? In: E. Perry, D. Collerton, F. LeBeau, & H. Ashton (Eds.), *New Horizons in the Neuroscience of Consciousness*. London: John Benjamins.

Volkan, V. D. (1984). Complicated mourning. *Annual of Psychoanalysis, 12*: 323–348.

Yovell, Y., Solms, M., & Fotopoulou, A. (2015). The case for neuropsychoanalysis: why a dialogue with neuroscience is necessary but not sufficient for psychoanalysis. *International Journal of Psychoanalysis, 96*: 1515–1553.

INDEX